H O P E

IN SUFFERING

**Letters from Peter
with Application
to the Coaching Profession**

Hope In Suffering
© 1993 by Full Court Press
P.O. Box 141513
Grand Rapids, Michigan 49514
ISBN 0-9634057-4-8

1 2 3 4 5 6 / 97 96 95 94 93
Printed in the United States of America

Cover photo courtesy of Athlon Publications

HOPE

IN SUFFERING

**LETTERS FROM PETER
WITH APPLICATION
TO THE COACHING PROFESSION**

Contents

Foreword • 7

Introduction to 1 Peter • 9

I. Hope in Suffering • 11
Coaching Clinic: Benefits of Suffering • 23
Prayer: Spiritual Warfare • 28

II. More Hope in Suffering • 29
Coaching Clinic: Goals • 39
Prayer: Waiting on the Lord • 44

III. Overcoming in His Steps • 45
Coaching Clinic: Motivation • 57
Prayer: Repentance • 60

IV. Righteous Relationships • 61
Coaching Clinic: God's Women in Coaching • 70
Prayer: Role Relationships • 76

V. Attitude in Adversity • 77
Coaching Clinic: Physical Fitness • 86
Prayer: Adversity • 89

VI. To Every Head Coach • 90
Coaching Clinic: Leadership • 99
Prayer: Team Morale • 111

Introduction to 2 Peter • 115

VII. Victory in Knowing Jesus • 117
  Coaching Clinic: The Athlete of the 90s •127
  Prayer: Seeking God's Coaching Job • 133

VIII. Faithful Living in Difficult Days • 135
  Coaching Clinic: The Authority of God's Word • 144
  Prayer: Strongholds • 151

IX. Return of the Lord • 153
  Coaching Clinic: Assurance and Sharing Christ • 160
  Prayer: Open Doors to Share Christ • 173

Appendices • 175

Appendix I: The Winning Run • 177

Appendix II: The Perfect Reliever • 181

Other Winning Run Foundation Materials • 187

Foreword

THE APOSTLE PETER has a message for coaches. It is a message of hope in suffering, and he is very qualified to speak on the subject. Most scholars believe Peter wrote his letters after the bloody Roman dictator, Nero, had come to power and persecution of Christians was breaking out, somewhere between 64—67 A.D. He spoke of hope in times of great stress. In that day, Christians weren't fired for losing ball games or despised by overzealous parents for not giving a teenager enough playing time. They were dressed in animal skins and fed to starving beasts for the enjoyment of a maddened crowd! That's stress with a capital "S!"

Peter would have been a good coach. His name means "rock-man." Jesus never gave Peter any special authority over other apostles or anyone else in the church. All believers are called "living stones" (1 Peter 2:5) and the church is built upon THE ROCK — Jesus Christ Himself. But the man who had once denied and deserted his "Head Coach" became a changed man on the inside. Once impetuous, Peter became patient. Once a crude, stumbling fisherman who always seemed to put his foot in his mouth, Peter became a wise encourager of others in the most extreme circumstances of life. Tradition says that when sentenced to execution by crucifixion, he requested to be hung upside down because he felt unworthy to die as Jesus had died. Such a man is worth listening to. Especially when his words are inspired by God's Holy Spirit! May our Lord Jesus Christ encourage and strengthen you in the most extreme trials as you study the letters of Peter.

Elliot Johnson

All Bible quotations are taken from the New International Version of God's Word, published by Zondervan Corporation, Grand Rapids, Michigan.

Introduction to First Peter

THIS BOOK is about suffering. It concerns a word that we coaches hate to hear: DEFEAT. But this book is also about Victory — the overwhelming VICTORY that is ours by faith in Jesus Christ. Since these words are directed to those who have trusted the Lord Jesus with their eternal destiny, any losses along the way are only *temporary* setbacks. For us, there is no such thing as *permanently* losing! Jesus Himself died for us and He has promised us eternal life (1 John 5:11—13). We know we'll win in the long run and that sustains us in the short run!

Do you relate to these words? Or has there never been a time in your life when you have trusted the Lord Jesus to save your soul from eternal loss? If not, turn to Appendix I and read The Winning Run right now. Until you give your life to Jesus Christ, you have no hope of comprehending the Word of God, for the Word of God is "spiritually discerned" (1 Corinthians 2:14).

Today, suffering and setbacks are as much a part of the Christian's life as they are of the unbeliever's life. In fact, a great man once said that whenever the Lord allows a wicked man to suffer, He allows a godly man to experience the same trial so He can demonstrate how to overcome in God's power! We suffer losses on the athletic field. We lose job opportunities, personal reputations, and material rewards. We hurt in relationships with players, family, and friends. Sometimes we feel anguish, pressure, failure, rejection, disappointment, and regret. Any number of circumstances can cause a flood of emotional hurt.

Can the Christian coach thrive in spite of losses? Certainly! We know that our God is working out everything for our ultimate good (Romans 8:28). He has given us power to walk day by day through the most severe trials. He desires to bless us (Psalm 1) and will do so in His time. Let us press on day by day, encouraged by His Word and by others who have overcome in His Name!

9

I. Hope in Suffering

DICKIE THON is no stranger to suffering. A Christian player, he was severely injured when hit in the eye by a pitched ball several years ago. By God's grace, Dickie has come back to play shortstop on the major league level.

1 Peter 1:1-7

Strangers in the World (verse 1) • **13**
Elected and Chosen (verses 1, 2) • **14**
The Trinity at Work (verse 2) • **15**
Praise—the Key to Overcoming
　(verses 3—5) • **17**
Yet Suffering Grief (verse 6) • **19**
Why? (verse 7) • **21**

☆ ☆ ☆ ☆ ☆ ☆
Coaching Clinic • The Benefits of Suffering
☆ ☆ ☆ ☆ ☆ ☆

Benefits of Suffering • **23**
How to Help Players Who Suffer • **25**
Never Give Up • **27**
War in the Heavenlies • **28**
Prayer: Spiritual Warfare • **28**

Strangers in the World

. . . Strangers in the world, scattered throughout. . . .

(verse 1)

RICHIE ASHBURN didn't fit in very well with the 1962 New York Mets. But he was sold to them by the Cubs, even though he was a .308 lifetime hitter. The expansion Mets became known for their ineptitude, while Ashburn was known as the complete ballplayer. Richie was a legend playing on a team that became legendary for being the worst team ever! He batted .306 that year and retired at the end of the season.

It takes a lot of determination to excel when you are out of your element. After all, fish never do well on dry land! But Richie Ashburn proved it could be done in baseball and Christians constantly prove that we can excel on foreign soil as well. Peter, who had been beaten and faced death in Jerusalem under Herod, wrote to Jewish Christians who had been driven from their "home field" in Jerusalem into Asia Minor and to Gentiles who had believed in Jesus because of their witnessing. They no longer fit into the pagan culture around them. Yet, they prospered in faith.

As believers in Jesus, we are all aliens and strangers on this planet (1 Peter 1:17, 2:11). As travelers through a strange land, we often think of our heavenly home. "For here, we don't have an enduring city, but we are looking for the city that is to come" (Hebrews 13:14). Philippians 3:20 says, "But our citizenship is in heaven. And we eagerly await a Savior from there, the Lord Jesus Christ." Any person living for Jesus is sometimes ostracized from the crowd. After all, the crowd in Jesus' home town tried to kill him by pushing Him off a cliff (Luke 4:28—30). He said He had no place on earth to "lay his head'" (Luke 9:58). We certainly can sometimes expect no better treatment if we truly represent Him!

Christians have been scattered before and God has used their suffering to spread the gospel of His love and forgiveness. If He does it again, may we do the same.

13

1. This sinful world is not the permanent home of the Christian.
2. We have citizenship in heaven!
3. We can expect to be ostracized at times for our commitment to Christ.
4. When Christians have been driven from their homes in the past, the gospel has advanced.

---

1 Peter 1:1, 2

Elected and Chosen

To God's elect . . . chosen according to the foreknowledge of God.

(verse 2)

IT'S A GREAT THRILL to be chosen as a professional baseball team's number one pick in the draft. And it's an even greater thrill to be the very first player chosen overall. Ex-pro catcher Jack King is probably the only man in history to have *two* sons chosen by pro teams in the first round. One son, Jim, was selected number one by Philadelphia in January, 1982, and his younger son, Jeff, was the first player chosen in 1986, having been picked by the Pirates.

While it is a thrill to be chosen in the baseball draft or even in a pick-up game, it is even more thrilling to think of being chosen by God Himself! Because Peter is writing to God's elect (His chosen ones), let's think about the implications. We are dealing with concepts from God's viewpoint, so a final explanation is impossible from our limited viewpoint.

God has a right to plan ahead for the future. Some call these plans His *decrees*. He decreed that He would create the universe and He created it. He decreed the laws of gravity, inertia, and thermodynamics. He decreed that man would be permitted to sin and that He would send a Savior to die for us. He decreed that He would save all who came to Him

14

by faith in that Savior, Jesus Christ! His invitation to "whosoever will" (Revelation 22:17) is "Come to Me" (Matthew 11:28). All who come find they are God's chosen people from the very "creation of the world" (Ephesians 1:4).

Some people object to God having a plan. They are happy to see men have plans and to carry them out, but they deny God that right in His own universe! But God is able to carry out every one of His plans, for He knows everything. That is His foreknowledge. He is God, after all!

So relax, Christian. If you are chosen by God and if He is working out His plan in your life, the suffering you endure has purpose. You may not know all the reasons why things happen — but you will some day! Eternity will reveal *everything.* You will then praise Him for every trial. Why not start now?

HOPE IN SUFFERING

1. Suffering is not by chance for the Christian.
2. God has a plan for your life and a purpose for your suffering.
3. God is not finished with you.
4. You can accept your circumstances because you know God is more wise than you are.

---

1 Peter 1:2

The Trinity at Work

. . . who have been chosen according to the foreknowledge of God the Father, through the sanctifying work of the Spirit, for obedience to Jesus Christ and sprinkling by His blood.

(verse 2)

THOUGH ALL MEMBERS of a football team are equally important, there exists a clear division of labor among them. For this reason, they practice different techniques in different groups. Offensive linemen are to block, running backs carry the football, quarterbacks throw, and receivers catch the ball. Defensive players tackle and break up pass plays. All are part of the team, but all perform different functions for the team.

Peter reveals that there is also a division of labor among the three personalities of the Godhead. While many cults (Jehovah's Witnesses and Mormons for example) deny the existence of the Trinity, Peter and other New Testament writers make it clear that our God is a "three-in-one" God. Each member of the "Trinity" has a different function.

God the Father planned your salvation. He had each of us in mind when He decreed that He would save everyone who came to Christ (Ephesians 1). He planned to send the Savior to redeem us before we were even called.

The Father's plan is to save us through the sanctifying work of the Holy Spirit. The Spirit is the one who seals us, "guaranteeing our inheritance" (Ephesians 1:13, 14). And He works mightily within us to bring us to maturity while here on earth! How important it is to let God's Spirit develop our lives so we won't stand in God's presence one day as "baby" Christians! Let's grow up!

Finally, the blood of Jesus Christ is the means of our salvation. Jesus, the Son of God, took upon Himself a body, living among men so we would know what God is like. He died in our place. When He shed His blood, He made a way for us to be acceptable to the Father! When we trust that blood sacrifice, all our sins are removed forever. Hebrews 9:22 says, "Without the shedding of blood there is no forgiveness." First John 1:7 says, "But if we walk in the light, as he is in the light, we have fellowship with one another, and the blood of Jesus, His Son, purifies us from all sin." We don't need to worry! Jesus has justified us and His blood keeps on cleansing us!

These words are the basis of Peter's encouragement in all kinds of suffering. Because of the work of the Trinity, we are chosen, set apart, and purified. We enjoy God's grace and resulting peace in abundance!

HOPE IN SUFFERING

1. We have much hope because of the work of the Trinity.
2. All God's work is by grace.
3. Because of His grace we have peace with God.
4. Having experienced grace, we can be graceful with others.
5. Our peace is not dependent upon outward circumstances.

---

1 Peter 1:3—5

Praise — the Key to Overcoming

Praise be to the God and Father of our Lord Jesus Christ!

(verse 3)

EVERYONE who has ever trusted Christ for salvation has great reason to praise the Lord. God has persisted, not only in getting His message to us, but also in keeping us. Ex-major leaguer Clint Hurdle has this testimony of how God saved him:

"I can remember coming into (baseball) chapel, just out of the shower, towel around my hair, getting my uniform on, halfway listening to the message. It was Mike Blaylock. He delivered the gospel message, the good news of Jesus Christ. I had kind of heard this story before but he knew it real good. At the end of the service he gave the opportunity for anyone who did not have a personal relationship with Jesus Christ to say the prayer. I can remember putting my head down and thinking, now would be the time, I've given everything else a chance . . . no. Not yet. There are a couple of things I haven't tried.

I did not pray that prayer of salvation until 1983 at the age of 26. I ran around a lost soul for eight years. When you saw my picture on the cover of *Sports Illustrated,* if that young man would have died in a car wreck he would have

17

spent eternity in hell. You can take it to the bank. There's a million guys like me down there, that the world thinks has it all together. The world by the tail, but they're losing their souls."

Like Clint Hurdle, all believers can praise the Lord for His great mercy shown to us. He has given us "new birth" in Jesus Christ and because He rose from the dead we have a *living* hope! Remember, Peter (who frequently wrote of the resurrection) is writing to Christians who had been driven from their earthly homes. They looked to their future heavenly homes, something that American Christians do less frequently because of our present comfort. But when we suffer, we are compelled to focus on eternity. We think on our spiritual wealth — an inheritance that can never perish. This means it is permanent. Fire or rust cannot harm our heavenly wealth. Unlike good food, it cannot be spoiled by mold or insects. And it will never fade like a bad stock market investment. No enemy can steal our assets because they are *KEPT* in heaven for you by God Himself. Our ultimate possession of Heaven and the treasures we have "sent on ahead" is secure.

And we ourselves? We are "shielded" by God's power. The word is a military term meaning "to garrison within a city." Operation Desert Shield protected Saudi Arabia from Iraqi invasion. But God's power shields Christians much more effectively and permanently. For this we praise and thank Him!

HOPE IN SUFFERING

1. This world is not our permanent home.
2. Our inheritance can never perish, spoil, or fade.
3. Because Jesus arose, we have a living hope.
4. We are shielded by the power of God.

Yet Suffering Grief

In this you greatly rejoice, though now, for a little while, you may have had to suffer grief in all kinds of trials.

(verse 6)

OREL HERSCHISER became the ace of the Los Angeles Dodgers pitching staff during the late 1980s. But in April, 1990, Orel had shoulder surgery, which ended his season. He faced the ordeal with much faith.

"The mental part about it for me is not a problem because I can deal with what has happened, Herschiser said. "The same God that was there when I knelt on the ground after beating the Mets in the seventh game of the playoffs, the same God that was there when I looked to the sky when we won the World Series, is here with me today. I'm going to make it."

Yet in May, 1991, after months of rehab and working short stints, he said, "If I allowed myself to think about what I've been through and all the different things that have happened and how much we've worked, then I would probably break down and just start crying."

Clearly the way back had been difficult and full of grief for Orel Herschiser. Dr. Clyde Narramore, the dean of Christian psychologists, suggests that grief might be called the common emotion. Evidently Peter was well aware of the emotion of grief for he wrote to believers who were experiencing much of it themselves. Verse 6 is the key verse in his entire letter, though the fact that God develops maturity and character in us through suffering is not a popular teaching today. Contrary to many false teachers, there is nothing wrong with our faith if we're suffering. It is merely God's method of perfecting us. Paul wrote, "For our light and momentary troubles are achieving for us an eternal glory that far outweighs them all" (2 Corinthians 4:17). He called our suffering light and momentary in comparison to eternity. Our problems are indeed temporary — never longer than necessary to produce God's desired results in us. For this we can rejoice and be thankful.

Peter mentioned "all kinds of trials." It's not that we face just one trial, but at times we face them in many forms and from different directions. We feel caught in a crossfire. Physical and emotional problems affect our spiritual lives. We all face everyday problems, but like Peter's audience we often face extreme circumstances that would undo us if we didn't keep our eyes on the Savior.

How can we handle so much suffering? It is important to share burdens. A Christian pastor or a friend who will keep matters confidential can often help by listening. Just talking it out helps us to arrive at the best course of action. Let your friends help you.

Ask God to show you His purposes. He is trustworthy. He loves you. Jeremiah 29:11 says that, "His thoughts for you are good and not evil, to give you a future and a hope." Remember to stay in Scripture. When you are grieving, many times certain verses seem to be just for you at that time.

God hears and answers prayer. Never forget to pray, whether you feel like it or not. Tell Him exactly where you hurt and how badly. He is the Great Physician.

Well-written Christian books and magazines can often help. And Christian music will elevate your spirits as it did when David's harp relieved Saul's depression long ago.

Sometimes developing a new interest keeps our mind off ourselves and our problems. And helping someone else helps us to bear our own load much better. Take a close look at your health habits. Grief seems to make us eat sporadically and unwisely, exercise inadequately, and not to rest properly. There is great hope for you as a Christian and you must not neglect caring for the temple God has given you.

Above all, seek the face of God. Ask Him what He is teaching you through the situation. The greatest tragedy would be to waste these precious trials! He has a purpose and a plan and you will be greatly blessed in the end!

1. O̶u̶r̶ ̶s̶u̶f̶f̶e̶r̶i̶n̶g̶ ̶i̶s̶ ̶o̶n̶l̶y̶ ̶t̶e̶m̶p̶o̶r̶a̶r̶y̶
2. O _____ t
   fu _____
3. Y _____ are
   su
4. T _____ out,
   th
5. S _____ sin
   or

---

1 Peter 1:

*These hav _____ than
gold, whi _____ ay be
proved ge _____ honor
when Jes*
_____ erse 7)

AFTER GOLD is mined, it is placed in a red-hot furnace. The purpose is not to destroy it but to purify it of the impurities, which float to the top and are easily skimmed off. The pure gold that remains is of great value.

God uses severe trials to refine His people today. When He "turns up the heat," it is never to destroy us, but to perfect us. He wants pure character and He will have it! Remember, we are not talking of life's common problems, but about persecution unto death. Peter knew that crucifixion was ahead of him. Yet, he had joy independent of his circumstances.

All of God's children experience His testing, refinement, and purification. Hebrews 12:8 tells us that if we do not experience God's discipline we are not a child of God! There are no shortcuts to maturity of character. The trial of our faith is the *only* way. It is His method and His school of hard knocks."

Our faith is of much greater value than gold! Faith turns sound doctrine into victorious living. Gold does not increase and multiply in the fire like faith does. Gold will perish one day, but faith never perishes. Faith results in praise, glory and honor, but gold is a metal which even the ungodly may possess.

Sometimes we are tempted to ask, "Why?" when the trials become severe. Jesus asked the same question on the cross. We may not know the final answer until we get to Heaven, but we do know that our trials are refining and purifying us. When the Lord Jesus reappears, we will thank God for all our trials. We may wish we had experienced more of them, for we will see all the reasons and their eternal value!

HOPE IN SUFFERING

1. Trials give us the opportunity to prove we have genuine faith.
2. Trials will result in great praise when Jesus is revealed.
3. Let us not become too introspective. Look to the God who has a glorious future planned ahead for us.
4. Faith is much more precious than gold.

The Benefits of Suffering

AS WE STUDY the Word of God, it becomes apparent that God's choicest servants have often suffered. Joseph, David, Paul, and the Lord Jesus all experienced great trials. Indeed, the Bible promises suffering to the Christian (2 Timothy 3:12, 1 Thessalonians 3:3, 4), teaches that suffering is often in the will of God (1 Peter 4:12—19), and cites our Lord as an example of suffering (1 Peter 2:19—23). We suffer physically, mentally, or emotionally and at times our suffering may be in all three areas! We may suffer guilt as a result of our own sin or false guilt from Satan, who tries to hamstring the child of God with his evil accusations. We may suffer a wounded spirit from the attacks of others and may need the deep, personal healing that only the Great Physician can perform.

Since suffering for the Christian is real and unavoidable, and because God is sovereign, He must have tremendous purposes in it for us! Though we can neither understand nor explain all suffering, we do know of some of its benefits. Let us examine several of these:

1. When we suffer we are crowded to Christ and His Word. We are forced to rely totally upon His strength and provision and not our own! In extreme suffering, only God can carry us through.

2. Character traits are produced in Christian suffering. Romans 5:3—5 says that ". . . suffering produces perseverance; perseverance, character; and character, hope . . .." Therefore, we should actually rejoice in suffering (Romans 5:3, James 1:2—4)!

3. When we suffer and accept it with thanksgiving (Ephesians 5:20, James 1:2), our faith in the sovereignty and goodness of God is proven. Suffering is beneficial because it proves our faith. The tested is always better than the untested.

23

4. Through suffering we understand the feelings of others who suffer in a world filled with evil. We are better able to empathize with those who hurt because we know how it feels to suffer.

5. Through suffering we experience and understand the grace of God. He gives us more grace to endure as needed. When we suffer because of the evil deeds of others, we see the grace of God toward them and learn to forgive as we have been forgiven.

6. When we suffer unjustly, God is glorified (1 Peter 1:7, 2:19—21). As we accept the trials placed upon us, others see how we have responded and give Him the glory He deserves. We must remember that His glory — not our comfort— is to be our purpose for living.

7. Finally, if we suffer in this life, we will appreciate Heaven so much more (Romans 8:18). How great it will be to be in the presence of Jesus, where there is no sin or suffering of any kind! For the believer, all suffering is temporary and lasts only a "little while" (1 Peter 5:10). When Jesus comes it will be over forever. Even so, come Lord Jesus!

How to Help Players Who Suffer

SOMETIMES our own pain is so large we have trouble reaching out to help others. And sometimes when we reach out to others in need, our own problems diminish in proportion. Just as we receive God's comfort in adversity, we will want to reach out to those close to us who also suffer. Doing so often speeds our own emotional healing!

Helping others is not easy. Some problems may not be "fixed" in this life. But suffering can draw us closer to God and to each other. In his book, *Why Would a Good God Allow Suffering?*, Kurt De Haan gives the following suggestions to those who would reach out to help others through their grief:

- Don't wait for someone to act first.
- Be physically present with them if possible and touch their hand or give an appropriate hug.
- Focus on their needs and not on your own discomfort with not having adequate answers.
- Allow them to express their feelings. Don't condemn their emotions.
- Learn about their problem.
- Don't pretend that you never struggle.
- Keep your words brief.
- Avoid saying, "You shouldn't feel that way," or, "You know what you should do."
- Assure them of your prayers.
- Pray! Ask God to help you and them.
- Keep in touch.
- Help them dispel false guilt by assuring them that suffering and sin are not inseparable twins.
- Help them find forgiveness in Christ if they are suffering due to sin, or if they become aware of some sin as they reflect on their lives.
- Encourage them to recall God's faithfulness in times past.
- Focus on Christ's example and help.
- Remind them that God loves us and cares for us and that He is in control.

- Encourage them to take one day at a time.
- Encourage them to reach out for the help they need (friends, family, pastor).
- Help them to realize that coping with troubles takes time.
- Remind them of God's shepherding love (Psalm 23).
- Remind them of God's control over the universe, both the big and small events of live.

"Rejoice with those who rejoice, and weep with those who weep."

— Romans 12:15

- Don't ignore their problem.
- Don't be artificial in trying to "cheer them up." Be genuine. Be the friend you were to them before trouble hit.
- Show them the love you would like other people to show you if you were in their situation.
- Be a good listener.
- Acknowledge how much they hurt.
- Give them time to heal. Don't rush the process.

Coach, let's not stand on the sidelines. Your players need you and you need to help them.

NEVER GIVE UP

It takes a little courage and a little
Self control,
And some grim determination if you
Want to reach a goal.
It takes a deal of striving and a firm
And stern set chin,
No matter what the battle, if you're
Really out to win.

There's no easy path to glory, there's
No rosy path to fame;
Life, however we may view it, is no
Simple parlor game.
But its prizes call for fighting, for
Endurance and for grit,
For a rugged disposition, and a don't
Know-when-to-quit.

You must take a blow or give one, you
Must risk and you must lose,
And expect that in the struggle you
Will suffer many a bruise.
But you mustn't whine or falter if a
Fight you once begin;
Be a man and face the battle — that's the
Only way to win!

—Author Unknown

War in the Heavenlies

IF YOU ARE a Christian coach and you are committed to be a dynamic influence upon others by verbally recommending Jesus Christ, you can expect opposition. While the Bible tells us that our God is all-powerful, all-knowing and everywhere present, it also teaches that He has temporarily allowed Satan to be "the prince and power of the air, the spirit now at work in those who are disobedient" (Ephesians 2:2).

Our Father has commissioned us to invade Satan's territory, to bind him in prayer, and to rescue those held "captive to do his will" (2 Timothy 2:26). War in the heavenlies is declared! American Christians are becoming more aware each day of tremendous spiritual conflict as the political, economic, educational, and even formal religious systems have turned away from God.

We must learn to wage war with the spiritual weapon of prayer, led by the Holy Spirit, if we are to overcome. Authors such as Mark Bubek (The Satanic Revival) and Frank Peretti (This Present Darkness) have alerted us to the power of doctrinal prayer warfare.

Coaches must learn to wage war for the cause of Christ against spiritual enemies that hamper their personal lives, their teams, and their schools. The prayers written at the end of each chapter of this book are designed to help. The words are not magic, but when prayed boldly in the power of the Holy Spirit, God will honor these prayers and changes will take place.

Let us never forget: We are at war with unseen spiritual forces. It's "swords drawn" all the way to the gates of heaven.

Prayer Warfare

Father,

Teach me to wage prayer warfare in the power of your Holy Spirit as I read your Word and consider your principles.

In the Name of Jesus, Amen.

II. More Hope in Suffering

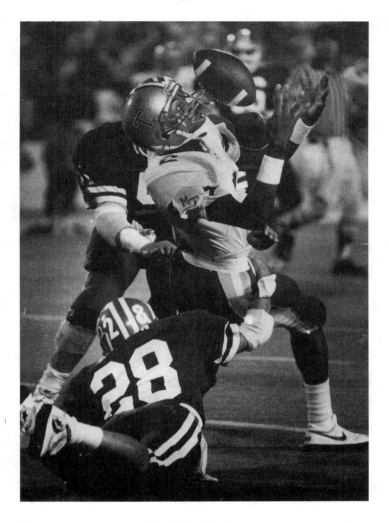

WE DON'T KNOW all the reasons why we suffer. But if we accept whatever comes our way, God can do great things in our lives.

1 Peter 1:9-24

The Goal: Our Great Salvation (verses 8, 9) • **31**
Glory Follows Suffering (verses 10—12) • **32**
Preparation for Action (verses 13—16) • **34**
The Impartial Judge (verses 17—22) • **36**
Men and Grass (verses 22—25) • **38**

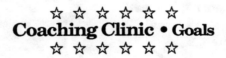

☆ ☆ ☆ ☆ ☆ ☆
Coaching Clinic • Goals
☆ ☆ ☆ ☆ ☆ ☆

Goals and Goal Setting • **39**
Principles of Goal Setting • **40**
Personal Goal Sheet • **42**
Team Goal Sheet • **43**
Prayer: Waiting on the Lord • **44**

The Goal: Our Great Salvation

Though you have not seen Him, you love him; and even though you do not see him now, you believe in him and are filled with an inexpressible and glorious joy; for you are receiving the goal of your faith, the salvation of your souls.

(verse 9)

FROM 1971 UNTIL 1974, the UCLA Bruins under coach John Wooden never lost a game. In 1973, they broke the record of 61 consecutive wins set by San Francisco in 1957. Their streak was not stopped until January 19, 1974, when Notre Dame beat them, 71-70. They had won an astonishing 88 consecutive games!

A Christian who is walking by the power of God's Spirit has great joy today. Why? Because he is winning much more than a string of basketball games. Because of his belief in Jesus, he is receiving *salvation!* This salvation is explained in three tenses. First, salvation is in the past tense because He *has given* us new birth (verse 3). Second, it is present tense because we *are being shielded* by God's power (verse 5). Third, our salvation is yet future, for it *will be revealed in the last time* (verse 5). All of this is reason for our inexpressible joy in spite of external circumstances. In coaches' terms: *we have won, we are winning,* and *we will win!* The suffering Christians to whom Peter wrote were on the losing side in the world's measurement of things, but were winning the only game that counts — the game of life.

Do you ever wonder how to identify a true Christian? There are a lot of professing Christians who only identify with Christ because it is the cultural thing to do. Some only attend church to discuss business deals. Maybe they are really deceived into thinking they are safe from God's coming wrath. Even some preachers merely preach for profit (1 Corinthians 2:17). But a true Christian has a deep love for the Lord Jesus and inexpressible joy coming from the inside. This love and joy are produced by the indwelling Holy

Spirit. True faith of real Christians is demonstrated and deepened by suffering. False faith is abandoned during trials. The person who merely professes Christianity will wash out during persecution.

The ultimate goal of our faith is the salvation of our souls. No pursuit in life, whether it be career, money, championships or any other relationship, is as important as our soul's salvation. Isn't it great to know that Jesus has won that salvation? The joy and encouragement of knowing Him gives great power to overcome the worst suffering.

HOPE IN SUFFERING

1. A Christian has supernatural power to rejoice in trials.
2. Love and joy distinguish a believer in Jesus from an unbelieving pretender.
3. Everything else is secondary to the salvation of our soul.
4. The goal of our faith is the salvation of our souls.

---

1 Peter 1:10—12

Glory Follows Suffering

Concerning this salvation, the prophets, who spoke of the grace that was to come to you, searched intently and with the greatest care, trying to find out the time and circumstances to which the Spirit of Christ in them was pointing when he predicted the sufferings of Christ and the glories that would follow.

(Verses 10, 11).

MANY COACHES who have experienced great success on one level have experienced much difficulty during stints at lower levels. For example, the Bills' Marv Levy had only a 45-60 record as a college coach, and the 49er's George Seifert was only 6-18. Both the Giants' Bill Parnells and the Bengels' Sam Wyche were 3-8 in college jobs. Furthermore,

BYU's coach Lavell Edwards, who has a national championship to his credit, coached high school football for eight years without a winning season! These coaches know the suffering that preceded glory.

While glory after suffering is not guaranteed a football coach in the physical realm, the Christian who endures suffering *always* has glory to anticipate! Peter described this spiritual principle. When the Old Testament prophet Isaiah wrote of the suffering of the Messiah (Isaiah 53) and His glory (Isaiah 11), he didn't understand all that the Spirit was leading him to record! Likewise, when David wrote of Jesus' suffering (Psalm 22) and his glory (Psalm 110), he longed to fully understand the seeming contradiction. Some scholars thought there would be two messiahs! But it was not until Jesus came that men realized that God's plan was for glory to result from Messiah's suffering. Colossians 1:26, 27 tells us that this "mystery" was kept hidden for ages. Peter says that even angels long to "look into" God's good news (verse 12). Because of Jesus' suffering, many will glorify Him in Heaven. He will be satisfied that His sacrifice was worth it.

Glory through suffering was the path for the early Christians to whom Peter wrote and it is God's plan for our lives today. What an encouragement to know that every loss, every disappointment, and every heartache will result in great glory when Jesus Christ is revealed! We must thank God for all our trials, knowing His plan is the best plan. We may not see all the reasons now, but one day we may even wish He had sent us more trials! Our God has great plans for us. Trust Him. You will be better off for having suffered.

HOPE IN SUFFERING

1. God's grace is manifested in Jesus' suffering.
2. Suffering is only temporary for the Christian.
3. Glory is certain for the Christian.
4. Remember to thank God in and for every trial.

Prepare for Action

Therefore, prepare your minds for action; be self-controlled; set your hope fully on the grace to be given you when Jesus Christ is revealed. As obedient children, do not conform to the evil desires you had when you lived in ignorance. But just as he who called you is holy, so be holy in all you do; for it is written: "Be holy, because I am holy."

(Verses 13—16)

THERE IS NO substitute for thorough preparation in coaching. Tom Landry learned how important preparation was very early in his professional playing days. In his autobiography, he tells of his first pro start as a defensive back. It was against Coach Paul Brown's Cleveland Browns. The Browns had an all-time great in quarterback Otto Graham and a great receiver in Mac Speedie, who set a single-game league record for receiving against Landry! Tom writes, "I realized my own limitations. I conceded that it was impossible to succeed solely on skill, on emotion, or even on determination. Any success I ever attained would require the utmost in preparation and knowledge. I couldn't wait and react to my opponent. I had to know what he was going to do before he did it. With my 10.4 speed in the hundred, I could never cover a 9.6 receiver by running with him; but if I knew where he was going, I could be there when he arrived."

Because of all Christ has done for us, we now have great motivation to run the great race of faith. That race requires preparation. The same character traits necessary for athletic success are necessary to run the race of life. We must "prepare for action." Our mind-set must be one of readiness for whatever is to come. The Boy Scouts recognize this and their motto is, "Be prepared." The study of the Word of God and prayer are the best preparation for each day's trials.

Our hope is to be 100 per cent in the future God has for us. Many Christians seem to have forgotten that this wicked world is neither our friend nor our home. We are to live with eternal values in view. The Bible says, "Do not love the world or anything in the world. If anyone loves the world, the love of the Father is not in him (1 John 2:15). James 4:4 says, "You adulterous people, don't you know that friendship with the world is hatred toward God? Anyone who chooses to be a friend of the world becomes an enemy of God." We are not prepared to live unless our mind is set on eternal values.

Peter also tells us to be "self-controlled." There is no substitute for self-discipline. We will achieve nothing spiritually, physically, or mentally without discipline. Bobby Knight, a successful basketball coach, has explained the importance of discipline: "It has always been my thought that the most important single ingredient to success in athletics or life is discipline. I have many times felt that this word is the most ill-defined in all our language. My definition of the word is as follows: 1) Do what has to be done; 2) When it has to be done; 3) As well as it can be done; and 4) Do it that way all the time."

Next, Peter calls us "obedient" children. The only way to respond to our great loving Father in Heaven is to obey Him. We obey Him because of our love for Him for what He has done for us in Christ. We are "non-conformists" to the values and opinions of this fallen world and to our own evil desires. The old desires are past and we are to live in our new nature. We are to "be holy" in *all* we do. To be holy means "to be separated unto God." He is our joy, our Lord, and the only one whom we must please. We must evaluate everything we do, think, or say in relation to God.

The plans of God for us and the evil days in which we live are great motivation to live holy, obedient, and disciplined lives for the Savior. Let's get prepared for action. Our wonderful Savior deserves it.

1. He who would fail to prepare to live for God is preparing to fail.
2. There is no true victory in living without self-control (discipline).
3. This world is only temporarily our residence. Our real home is in Heaven.
4. Be a non-conformist to the evil ways of unbelievers.
5. God has separated us to Himself. Let's live for Him.

---

1 Peter 1:17—21

The Impartial Judge

Since you call on a Father who judges each man's work impartially, live your lives as strangers here in reverent fear. For know that it was not with perishable things such as silver or gold that you were redeemed from the empty way of life handed down to you from your forefathers, but with the precious blood of Christ, a lamb without blemish or defect. He was chosen before the creation of the world, but was revealed in these last times for your sake. Through him you believe in God, who raised him from the dead and glorified him, and so your faith and hope are in God.

(Verses 17—21)

MAKING GOOD JUDGMENTS on players' abilities and attitudes is crucial for a coach to be successful. It is important to be as impartial as possible, for naturally we will like some players more than others. However, the good coach never lets his personal tastes affect his judgment of a player's ability. He may neglect a great asset to the team. Neither can he afford to play a person just because he likes him. Also, a good coach can't overlook a bad attitude on the part of a player he likes. He risks much team dissention if he does overlook it.

Our God uses better judgment than the best coach in this world. He always judges impartially. He loves us all equally and His judgments are always fair. Peter says that He will one day judge our works. This judgment has nothing to do with being saved from Hell — that was accomplished for all who believe in Jesus' death and resurrection. But the fact that God will judge our works to determine the degree of our reward in Heaven should give us a reverent fear of the Lord which results in a "godly carefulness" in living. Someone has said that a wise man is known by what and whom he fears. It is very wise to fear a holy God!

Nothing is as meaningless as a life lived without God. J. Vernon McGee reminds us that everything in the universe (sun, moon, stars, plants and animals) serves a purpose. But man without God has no purpose or meaning in life. Jesus gave us purpose by redeeming us from the emptiness! We have a reason to live — to glorify and serve Jesus! And we have an impartial judge in whom to hope! God, who raised Jesus from the dead, will never let us down. Let us hope in Him. And let us faithfully serve Him!

HOPE IN SUFFERING

1. Because God raised Jesus, He will resurrect all who believe in Him.
2. God will judge our works impartially. He is fair to all.
3. Jesus gives us purpose for living.
4. Faith placed in God is well-placed faith.
5. Jesus' blood is precious, and it is applied to all believers!

Men and Grass

All men are like grass, and all their glory is like the flowers of the field; the grass withers and the flowers fall, but the word of the Lord stands forever.

(verse 24)

IF A PERSON LIVES to be 65 years of age, he will have about 600,000 hours of life to spend on earth. An average of eight hours a day is spent working or in school, 8 hours sleeping, and 8 hours for personal purposes. This makes for 200,000 hours in each category. When we compare the time spent doing what we really *want* to do, it seems very small, doesn't it? Pro golfer Lee Trevino comments on the temporary nature of earthly pursuits: "Fame is vapor, popularity is an accident, money takes wings. Those who cheer you today may curse you tomorrow. The only thing that endures is character."

As Christians, born again through the Word of God, Peter exhorts us to love each other deeply, from the heart. We may model body builders, coaches of great wealth or fame and powerful leaders in our profession, but all of us are withering, fading, dying creatures. Our days are numbered! They are not many in comparison to eternity, and what days we have are sometimes spent carelessly.

Someone has said that the only things that endure are the Word of God and the souls of men. If this is true, it makes much sense to love and to invest our days in these things.

How are you investing your days?

HOPE IN SUFFERING

1. God's Word and men's souls are eternal.
2. Money, sex and power are temporary.
3. If we are born again, we will love other Christians.
4. Everyone, whether wealthy or poor, can invest in eternal things.

Goals and Goal-Setting

IT IS VERY IMPORTANT for a person to be "goal-oriented." There is an old saying, "Aim at nothing and you'll hit it every time." We need one overall life goal or life purpose, intermediate goals (objectives) to take us in the direction of that goal, and a plan to reach each objective. The overall goal (purpose) for each born-again believer in Jesus must be *to glorify God and to enjoy our relationship with Him* every day. We do this by becoming like Jesus in every thought, word and deed. The fact that one day we will be like Him (Romans 8:29) means that when we make this our personal goal we are *winning* already!

Statistical goals merely measure success on a scoreboard or stat sheet. They can subtract concentration from this most important goal! Though goals seem to help some people more than others, they are valuable because: 1) They keep current attitudes and actions in line with ultimate purpose, 2) They give focus and clarity in decision-making, 3) They provide direction and a framework for action, and 4) They remind us of what is possible and point us forward.

Principles of Goal-Setting

IF GOALS are of value, how should they be selected? What are some valid guidelines for setting performance goals? Following are some criteria in establishing goals:

1. Goals should be written and kept at hand. They should list a certain attitude or achievement to be fulfilled by a specific time.
2. A goal must be reachable. Make it a challenge, but be realistic.
3. He who fails to plan, plans to fail. Include a plan which may have more than one part that will lead to the achievement of your goal. Then get busy. Plan your work and then work your plan.
4. Goals must be flexible. Be willing to change direction if it becomes evident there is a better way. (See James 4:13—17)
5. Set goals only in relation to those things over which you have control. You cannot control others' attitudes or actions. But you can control your own.
6. For maximum motivation, set only goals which are in line with your overall purpose in life. Anything outside your personal value system will make you double-minded and therefore unstable.
7. Few people can believe or achieve a goal they have never seen achieved by someone else. What model are you using to provide a picture of what success looks like? Jesus is your only valid model (Matthew 10:25).
8. Trophies, Awards, championships, statistical, and other self-satisfying goals easily take the place of your overall purpose. These goals then become detrimental to performance level! They rob you of concentration on the task at hand (Matthew 6:25—33).
9. Self-satisfying goals only motivate until something more self-satisfying (relief from pain, a bad experience, or fatigue) comes along. Self-satisfying goals cause tightening up under pressure because of a desire to appear in a good light or to please others. They take concentration from the task at hand and put it on self.

10. Identify your own purpose in life. This will aid consistency and bring all your goals into focus and prevent double-mindedness.

On the following page is a personal goal sheet for your use. Use it to establish goals and plans in each area of your life. Make sure every goal points directly toward your life purpose or it will cause conflict in your life. You may want to list goals under other categories than the six listed. Below is an example of a goal and plans under the "career" category:

Goal #5 (Career): To coach with excellence every day.

Plan:
1. Attend 2 clinics per year.
2. Work at 3 different camps per year to gain additional insight.
3. With a peer's help, evaluate all phases of my program each year.

Research shows it is important to set our own goals, and not to assume those someone else has set for us. Be creative and listen to God as He directs you.

Personal Goal Sheet

Life Purpose: To glorify God and to enjoy Him every day.

Goal #1   (Spiritual):_____

    Plan:
        1.
        2.
        3.

Goal #2 (Mental): _____

    Plan:
        1.
        2.
        3.

Goal #3 (Physical): _____

    Plan:
        1.
        2.
        3.

Goal #4 (Social): _____

    Plan:
        1.
        2.
        3.

Goal #5 (Career): _____

    Plan:
        1.
        2.
        3.

Goal #6 (Family): _____

    Plan:
        1.
        2.
        3.

Team Goal Sheet

(An example of a goal sheet for a baseball team. As "benevolent dictator" it is your job to help team members personalize the type of goals listed here if the team is to be effective. Feel free to add or subtract as you formulate your own team plan).

Team Purpose: To Achieve Maximum Team Potential

Goal #1: Every player placing team interests ahead of self-interest.

    Plan:

1. Be willing to bunt to move a runner.
2. Be willing to take pitch on steal.
3. Be willing to fulfill assigned role on the team.

Goal #2: Play every inning with an attitude of intensity.

    Plan:

1. Total mental concentration on your task at hand.
2. Total physical effort when called upon to perform.
3. Total emotional control and release at the appropriate times.

Goal #3: To develop personally to the maximum.

    Plan:

1. Be receptive to instruction.
2. Become a team leader as an upper-classman.
3. Present positive image of self and team to the public.

Waiting on the Lord

Father,

You have given us specific instructions to wait upon You when we lack specific direction. That's what I am doing right now. I come into Your presence for the purpose of waiting before You. I have no agenda, no plan of my own for overcoming the obstacles before me. I am against a stone wall that only You can move. Apart from your grace in my life, I am stymied and stuck.

You have told us to be still before the Lord and to wait patiently before Him. I am now still and waiting. My soul waits for You more than a nightwatchman waiting for the morning. You have commanded me not to fret, so I am relaxing in your greatness and your provision. You promised that they who wait upon the Lord would renew their strength, would mount up with wings as eagles, would run and not grow weary and walk and not be faint. I'm here to have my exhausted strength renewed by You in Your good time. Strengthen my heart as I wait upon You.

You are worthy of my hope and trust. Weeping may endure for a night, but joy comes in the morning. My hope is in You and I will yet find many more great reasons to praise You. I will be still and know that You are God.

In the Name of Jesus, Amen.

III. Overcoming in His Steps

NO ONE PROMISED the Christian that life would be easy. In fact, we are promised trials and suffering. The fact that we get dirty from it all means we've been in a battle that counts!

1 Peter 2

Grow (verses 1—3) • **47**
Rejected By Men (verses 4—8) • **49**
Chosen to Win (verses 9—12) • **50**
Respect for Authority (verses 13—17) • **52**
Suffering Unjustly (verses 18—20) • **54**
Jesus—Our Suffering Role Model
    (verses 21—25) • **55**

☆ ☆ ☆ ☆ ☆ ☆
Coaching Clinic: Motivation
☆ ☆ ☆ ☆ ☆ ☆

The Greatest Motivation • **57**
Two Ways of Coaching • **59**
Prayer: Repentance • **60**

Grow

Like newborn babies, crave pure spiritual milk, so that by it you may grow up in your salvation, now that you have tasted that the Lord is good.

(verses 2, 3)

BILL CURRY was an All-Pro center and played in three Super Bowls. He has been a college football coach at Georgia Tech, Alabama, and Kentucky. Bill says, "I walked down a church aisle to accept Christ when I was nine years old. I said all the right words. But growing up I went my own way. I made a lot of speeches. I lived a lot of hypocrisy." It was on a Holy Land tour that Bill decided to really grow up in the Lord. While visiting the Garden of Gethsemane, he quietly said to the Lord, "This is the place where the Master sweat blood for me." The Lord wouldn't let me forget the experience. I made a recommitment of my life on the spot."

Peter tells us what suffering is supposed to produce in our lives. Because we are born again, he encourages us to grow up by developing godly traits which please the Lord. When we were born again, it was an act of God in response to the faith we placed in Jesus Christ, His promised Messiah. But now, God expects His children to do something to grow spiritually. He tells us to "get rid of traits of our old evil nature: malice, deceit, hypocrisy, envy, and slander (verse 1). These things must be put off like a dirty shirt.

Examine each trait to be shed. First is malice. What is malice? It is congealed, persistent anger toward another person. Do you have bitterness in your heart and a chip on your shoulder? Then you have not put off malice and you must get rid of it before you can grow.

Next, deceit of all forms must go. How many times do you only tell the part of the truth favorable to you for a certain reason? That is deceit. We try to deceive others into thinking we're something we are not. Some people try to deceive their bosses into thinking they're doing an honest day's work. They work harder at deceit than they do at work! Some coaches are quick to blame their team when they themselves have made an error in judgment. How much better to own up to our failures. It's much easier for others to accept us despite our shortcomings than to tolerate deceitful behavior. Ask Richard Nixon!

Hypocrisy is attempting to pass ourselves off as something we are not. It must be confessed and forsaken as Bill Curry did.

What about envy? Envy is grieving at the welfare of someone else. Do you envy others — their jobs, their influence, their records, their players?

Do you speak evil of others to try to make yourself look good? Slander is another trait of the old nature that must be put off.

All of us who have been saved have tasted the goodness of the Lord. Now, we are to grow up in Him. As J. Vernon McGee says, "We need the total Word of God. It's great to find comfort in God's Word, but we don't grow by lifting out a verse for comfort now and then. We need a balanced diet of God's Word, for there is no growth apart from the pure spiritual milk of the Word of God. The Word of God never leaves us hungry as it feeds us."

Are you still a baby Christian needing to be patted and burped by another Christian all the time? Then get into the Word — and let the Word get into you!

OVERCOMING IN HIS STEPS

1. A believer craves God's Word — not man's programs or his opinions.
2. We are to separate ourselves from our old sinful ways.
3. We must study God's Word to grow. This means spending time in each section so it can truly control our lives in a balanced fashion.

Rejected By Men

As you come to him, the living Stone — rejected by men but chosen by God and precious to him . . .

(verse 4)

ON SEPTEMBER 27, 1980, Marvin Hagler defeated England's Alan Minter in London for the undisputed middleweight boxing championship of the world. But Hagler's fight wasn't over yet. Minter's rowdy fans launched a barrage of beer bottles with such vehemence that Hagler had to be smuggled out of the ring for his own safety — before he was even proclaimed the new champ!

Hagler wasn't the only champion to be rejected. Mankind has also rejected the only Son of God as Savior and King. And because of man's rejection of Jesus, they often reject His followers.

But we can take heart. Though Jesus was rejected by men, He is loved, chosen and precious to God! He is the very cornerstone of the spiritual house of God! An Old Testament story may help to understand what is happening. When Solomon's Temple was being constructed, the stones were cut to exact measurements at a quarry and assembled at the temple site (1 Kings 6:7). Tradition says that a fine-looking stone was sent to the builders at the beginning of the project. But they couldn't fit it in anywhere, so they pushed it over a hill to make room for others. It was in their way. Finally, they concluded the job and called for the cornerstone. Word came from the quarry, "We sent you the cornerstone at the very beginning!" Then they remembered the stone they had rejected and with great effort hauled it back and set it into place.

Jesus Christ is the very cornerstone of God's spiritual house. He is rejected today. But one day every knee will bow, accepting His right to rule as He is set up as King of all the world.

All believers in Jesus, no matter whether rejected by family, friends, or the public, are living stones in God's house (1 Peter 2:5). We are "elect" (1 Peter 1:1) and greatly valued by God (1 Peter 1:18)! He has made us kings and priests (1 Peter 2:5, 9; Hebrews 4:16). We need no mediator other than Jesus Himself to approach God directly!

Have you ever felt rejected because of your stand for Christ? You're in good company. Jesus was rejected. Millions of His followers are still rejected by the world. Remember, God accepts you. And His acceptance is the only one that ultimately matters.

OVERCOMING IN HIS STEPS

1. To be rejected by those who go the way of the world means you are in good company.
2. Those who trust Christ will never be sorry.
3. Those who don't trust the Cornerstone will be crushed by it.

---

1 Peter 2:9—12

Chosen to Win

But you are a chosen people, a royal priesthood, a holy nation, a people belonging to God, that you may declare the praises of him who called you out of darkness into his wonderful light.

(verse 9)

BOB PETTIT was a great basketball player for the St. Louis Hawks. He retired at the end of the 1964-65 season having scored 20,880 points over an 11-year career. He was a 10-time all-pro and the first NBA player to score 20,000 lifetime points.

It is a great thing to be gifted with the athletic ability of a Bob Pettit. But it's even greater to have been chosen by God spiritually, for that's exactly what Peter says we are! We think we have chosen Christ (and in a sense we have), but really He is the one who has chosen us (John 15:16). Every believer in Jesus is both loved and wanted! It doesn't matter what our background is, how many wins or losses we have, or how much or little money we have. We are chosen by God for His purposes — to glorify Him by winning in the game of life.

Peter also says we are a "royal priesthood." Because God opened the way to His presence by the death of Christ, all who are in Jesus are priests. We can come to God in prayer in Jesus' name with no need for another human "priest." This doesn't mean we can't pray for each other, for we should. But we can each go directly into God's throne room directly and individually.

Peter next writes that we are a "holy nation" and "a people belonging to God." Both Israel and the organized church have failed miserably in walking with God. But if you have a relationship with Jesus Christ, you are holy and belong to God! Whether you are Russian, German, Jewish, Chinese, American, black, white, brown or red you are a member of a great people whose God is the Lord. Psalm 144:15 says, "Blessed are the people whose God is the Lord."

What a great position we have in Christ! *He* is our righteousness before God! Though we are aliens in this world, we have a wonderful home in Heaven. We are chosen to win!

OVERCOMING IN HIS STEPS

1. All who know Jesus as Savior are chosen by God.
2. All believers have direct access to God through Christ.
3. Believers are to declare His praises by word and deed.
4. Believers are strangers and aliens in this world.
5. Though evil men will accuse us, our good deeds still glorify God.

Respect for Authority

Submit yourselves for the Lord's sake to every authority instituted among men: whether to the king, as the supreme authority or to governors, who are sent by him to punish those who do wrong and to commend those who do right.

(verses 13, 14)

FOR ELEVEN YEARS, Don DeVoe was a successful basketball coach at the University of Tennessee. But when he accepted an interim job at Florida in 1989-90 (the previous staff had gotten the Gators into trouble over rules violations), he experienced problems from the first day. Two players boycotted his first practice. Athletes used to getting whatever they wanted refused to respect his authority. He was mocked and ridiculed so badly that he decided not to seek the position permanently. The scandle-riddled Florida program lost a chance to hire a good coach because of the rebellion.

Just as athletes are to respect and submit to their coach's authority, all of us are under human government in this world. We will always have someone over us in our job. We are accountable to authority somewhere along the line. *Every* authority is to be respected for his position.

When Peter wrote to scattered Christians, a madman named Nero was the new emperor of Rome. There was no real justice. As today, the poor had no chance. The rich could always buy clever lawyers to evade the law. Roman law was the pride of their society. Yet, it was responsible for the crucifixion of Jesus and it persecuted the early Christians!

In modern America, where the preaching of God's Word is politely suppressed, are we to rebel? No. Let us obey the government unless it issues commands in direct opposition to God's stated commands, as when the Jewish religious rulers commanded Peter and John to stop talking about Jesus. They replied, "Judge for yourselves whether it is right in God's sight to obey you rather than God. For we cannot help speaking about what we have seen and heard" (Acts 4:19, 20).

When Christians submit to godly civil law, it silences ignorant men who criticize them. We are to submit for our own good and for the good of the society. After all, even a poor, inept government is better than no government at all. Can you imagine the chaos that would exist if there were no law of any kind?

What is the purpose of government? It is to punish those who do wrong and to commend those who do right (verse 14). Therefore, as coaches, our own job should be to oppose evil and to reward righteousness. We aren't talking about punishing a boy for missing a shot, fumbling a football, or hanging a curve. We are talking about breaking training rules, maintaining destructive attitudes, or bringing disgrace to the school. We must act appropriately.

As coaches, our bosses are to be respected. When the principal or athletic director make unwise decisions concerning our sport, they still deserve our respect because of their position. We are to maintain a submissive attitude. Our natural reaction when treated unfairly is to strike back. But God says, "Vengeance is mine; I will repay" (Romans 12:19). Jesus commanded us to forgive, and promised eternal rewards for all unjust suffering (Matthew 5:11, 12).

OVERCOMING IN HIS STEPS

1. We are to respect and submit to authority.
2. The purpose of authority is to punish evil and to reward righteous behavior.
3. Coaches must punish ungodly actions and attitudes and praise good deeds and attitudes.

53

Suffering Unjustly

For it is commendable if a man bears up under the pain of unjust suffering because he is conscious of God.

(verse 19)

THE UNIVERSITY OF MISSOURI football team suffered unjustly for the official's oversight in a 1990 Big 8 contest against Colorado. Down 31-27 late in the game, the Buffaloes scored from the one-yard line on the game's final play for a 33-31 victory. Controversy erupted immediately, as the final play was actually a 5th down allowed by the officials! Following a heated discussion with them, coach Bob Stull held out little hope for a correction of the mistake. "It was too late. When I talked to them, they didn't say much," Stull said.

All of us suffer unjustly during this life. Nobody knows which Missouri players and coaches accepted their grief because of a consciousness of God or because they had no choice. However, Peter writes that if Christians endure unjust suffering because of a God-consciousness, they are to be commended. Maybe we have been wrongly accused. Maybe we have been discriminated against because of the color of our skin or because of our social status or because we are a Christian. Maybe we have been unfairly criticized or even fired unfairly from a good job. Our natural reaction is to strike back. But God says, "Vengeance is mine; I will repay" (Romans 12:19). If we take unjust suffering as allowed by God for our ultimate good (Romans 8:28), God works in mighty power in our lives to bring about His desired results. Jesus promised eternal rewards for bearing unjust suffering (Matthew 5:11, 12).

God can be glorified in the most undesirable circumstances. Sometimes, the most dedicated to the Father suffer the most. In the early church, slaves and servants made up a high percentage of the congregation. Undeserved punishment and suffering was common. Bearing up under unjust suffering pleases God because it demonstrates His grace. Let us remember to bear all injustices in the knowledge that we serve a God who will one day right every wrong!

OVERCOMING IN HIS STEPS

1. We are sure to suffer unfairly in this life.
2. We must remain conscious of God when we suffer unfairly.
3. One day, God will right all wrongs by making all things new again.

---

1 Peter 2:21—25

Jesus—Our Suffering Role Model

To this you were called, because Christ suffered for you, leaving you an example, that you should follow in his steps.

(verse 21)

WHEN BRANCH RICKEY began the integration of professional baseball, he sought a man of great talent and character. He found such a person in Jackie Robinson. In detailed briefings, Mr. Rickey explained the unfair abuse Jackie would receive and empathized that he must not fight back or retaliate. "You're looking for someone too weak to fight back," Jackie replied. "I'm looking for someone with the strength *not* to fight back," said Mr. Rickey. Jackie Robinson became a hero, a role model in baseball, and a champion of his race.

We have an even greater role model in our Christian life, for Jesus Christ Himself gave us an example of how to endure unjust suffering. Certainly it is not His suffering for the sins of the world that is an example for us — that suffering is our redemption. We cannot suffer to wash away our sins. But His life on earth is our example. He spent 30 years suffering misunderstanding as a man. When He preached for 3 years, He suffered undue criticism from ignorant men. He never retaliated or threatened to retaliate. Instead, Jesus trusted His life to the God who judges justly. We are called upon to do the same. We know we will suffer unjustly. Take it as a truth: Life is unfair! Especially to the Christian. Coaches suffer from the criticism of ignorant fans, but we must trust that God is working out a higher purpose in it.

We suffer loss on the field of play. Motivation by revenge is entirely ungodly. As a man, Jesus' provocation to retaliate during his arrest, trial and crucifixion was extreme. How He must have wrestled with the thought of using His infinite power to stop such gross injustice. But He had a higher purpose. Our salvation would have been impossible if He had resisted the unfair treatment. Our motives in coaching must be to elicit only the best effort from each player. The revenge motive is not only wrong, it is ineffective over the long haul.

How do you respond to unjust suffering or unexpected loss?

OVERCOMING IN HIS STEPS

1. Because of sin, life is unfair, especially for the Christian.
2. Jesus' life is our only true role model.
3. We must not retaliate or ever threaten to get even.
4. Only God judges justly.
5. It is by Jesus' wounds that we are saved from our sin. Even so, unjust suffering serves an eternal purpose in our lives.

The Greatest Motivation

THE HIGHEST LEVEL of motivation was displayed by the Lord Jesus Christ. He faced the greatest obstacles known to man as He walked the earth for 33 years and then gave His life for our freedom from the tyranny of sin. Jesus was highly motivated in everything He did, or He didn't do it.

Jesus' ability to say "no" to sin was demonstrated by His victory over Satan's temptations following His 40 days of fasting in the wilderness. His intensity for the holiness of God was shown by His aggressive expulsion of the money-changers from the temple. His compassion for those who had lost loved ones was shown as He wept over Lazarus. But it is at Calvary that He showed His greatest motivation, as He endured the torture of crucifixion to purchase our salvation. The Lord Jesus had prior knowledge of Roman crucifixion. It was adopted by the empire as a crime deterrent, and the ugly remains of bodies were visible on crosses along roads around Jerusalem. Jesus knew that He was to be crucified at a certain time (Luke 9:22, 23).

After an illegal, all-night "mock trial," Jesus was beaten (Luke 22:63, 64). A "crown" of thorns was pressed into His head (Matthew 27:29, 30). He was spat upon (Matthew 27:30) and whipped (Matthew 27:26). The Roman scourge had several thongs with sharp bone or stone tied in the ends. By the time a brutal soldier finished whipping a victim, the back was so ripped that the man appeared "skinned alive."

Once at the site of crucifixion outside Jerusalem, Jesus' arms were stretched along a beam and spikes were driven between the carpal bones of His wrists. A spike was also driven through His feet, fastening them to a vertical pole. The body weight of an average man in this position was often sufficient to dislocate both shoulders. Jesus' lungs were compressed and His breathing passages constricted. Many victims of crucifixion suffocated to death. When one being crucified pulled his body up to gasp for air (causing great pain in his hands and feet), he would soon drop his full body weight causing further agony. Cicero, a Roman politician who lived in the century before the birth of Jesus, wrote that crucifixion was the most cruel and horrible of all tortures.

What Motivated our Savior to this extreme in human suffering? His motivation was His Love for you and me. He could have called it all off and justly annihilated all mankind, but He loved us too much to ever give up God's plan for our redemption. Only by His death could He pay for our sin. Only Love could motivate the sacrifice He made. And this selfless love is ours when He enters our heart!

Two Ways of Coaching

THERE REALLY ARE only two value systems represented by coaches. A coach who is committed to Jesus Christ and walking by faith in God by the power of His Spirit has one set of priorities. One who adopts the world's value system, based upon self-serving motives, has another. It is well to consider the following chart and determine where you fit as a coach:

	WORLD'S VALUE SYSTEM	GOD'S VALUE SYSTEM
Goals	Trophies, rings, prestige, money.	Develop maximum potential of God-given abilities.
Orientation	Self-centered	Centered on Jesus Christ
Motivation	Self-glorification	Glory of God
Methods	Dominate others	Serve others Love for Others
Power	Old human nature	The Holy Spirit
Attitude	Self-confident independence	Confident dependence on God
Results	Performances short of capacity	Achieve maximum potential of players and team.

Repentance

Dear Father,

I confess my personal sins as You bring them to my remembrance. These include the sin of coaching according to the world's value system at times. I promise to confess other sins as You point them out to me. Thank You that You have "destroyed him who had the power of death, that is the devil." I submit to Your Lordship in every area of my life and rest under the covering of Your mighty hand. Please protect me and my family from physical harm each day whether we are together or apart. Please protect us from emotional damage caused by those who mean evil to us or from those who mean well but are ignorant of our needs. Please protect us from spiritual indifference and destruction which we see destroying so many around us.

Protect us from bad decisions concerning careers, who our children will date and marry, financial matters, and where we attend church. Protect our children from negative peer pressure and from the lust of the flesh which can destroy this body.

I confess the sins of our nation: violent sins of robbery, murder, and rape; sexual sins of fornication, adultry and homosexuality; religious sins of unbelief, legalism, and self-righteousness; lifestyle sins of gluttony, obesity, and drunkenness; political sins of bribery, injustice, and dishonesty; educational sins of pride, arrogance, and indifference to the needs of others; business sins of greed, lust, and selfishness; and family sins of divorce, child abuse, and lack of love. Lord, have mercy on us and save our country.

I praise You, Lord Jesus Christ, that You have been here on this earth, lived completely above and apart from all sin, died on our behalf, rose again, and ascended into Heaven. I claim the shelter of Your precious blood to protect and cover us from all accusations of the enemy.

In the Name of Jesus, Amen.

IV. Righteous Relationships

GODLY FEMALE COACHES are needed to train girls to perform and to live like the ladies God wants them to become. Every relationship must honor Him.

The Yow Sisters

"I see my job as an opportunity to minister. I love sports and I love the Lord. I see my job as more than coaching. I want to be able to minister through coaching."

Susan Yow, *Women's Basketball Coach*
Kansas State University

"The main thing is to be a good steward. You should take the opportunities when they're available."

Debbie Yow, *Athletic Director*
St. Louis University

"We want them (others) to see that our relationship with Christ is vital, that it's exciting and alive, and that we depend on it."

Kay Yow, *Women's Basketball Coach*
North Carolina State University
1988 Olympic
Women's Basketball Coach — Gold Medalist

1 Peter 3

The Value of a Good Assistant (verses 1—6) • **63**
The Head Coach and Commitment (verse 7) • **64**
Repaying Evil with Good (verses 8—16) • **66**
When Suffering is God's Will (verses 17—22) • **68**

☆ ☆ ☆ ☆ ☆ ☆
Coaching Clinic: God's Women in Coaching
☆ ☆ ☆ ☆ ☆ ☆

God's Woman in the Coaching Profession • **70**
Example • **75**
Prayer: Role Relationships • **76**

The Value of a Good Assistant

Wives, in the same way be submissive to your husbands.

(verse 1)

GOOD ASSISTANT COACHES are valuable, even indispensable to a winning team. When an assistant is loyal and submissive to the head coach, harmony and efficiency is the result. The same happens in a marriage. The Bible says that he who finds a wife finds a good thing (Proverbs 18:22). God says that she is to be submissive to her husband. The Lord does not say she must submit to men in general, but to her own husband, as Sarah submitted to Abraham, calling him "master" (Genesis 18:12). The result could be the changed life of the husband! Desirable character traits include purity, reverence, and a gentle and quiet spirit, which are of great worth in God's sight (verses 2, 4).

What a challenge for female coaches. It is probably more difficult for a woman who must "command her troops" all day during school and practice to come home and be submissive to her husband. But it is imperative. It's a matter of recalling God's assigned role in each case. As a head coach, a lady must be an assertive leader, but as a wife she is to be a submissive supporter of her husband. Because suffering had produced Christian character in the women to whom Peter wrote, they were able to respond properly in the home. That's the teaching in Chapter 3. Peter is writing to women in a tough situation. Many were married to unsaved husbands. (In Ephesians 5, Paul had written to Christian marriages where husband and wife were spirit-filled believers.) To marry an unsaved husband is a major mistake and God warns us against it (2 Corinthians 6:14). But if a wife accepts Christ after marriage, she is to stay married and try to win her husband by her behavior. As Vernon McGee says, "she is to be a good assistant, submitting to him unless asked to do anything which would dishonor the Lord Jesus."

Certainly she is not to dishonor God. For example: if her husband wanted her to visit a lewd nightclub, dress seductively in public, rob a bank, or use or transport drugs for him, she is clearly to please the Lord in all things, and these would not please Him. But a Christian wife is a supportive assistant to her husband. And she has great influence as she does what is right at home.

RIGHTEOUS RELATIONSHIPS

1. Wives are to be good assistants to husbands.
2. Outer adornment must not exceed inner beauty.
3. God values a gentle and quiet spirit.
4. Wives have much influence. They can win their husbands without a word.

---

1 Peter 3:7

The Head Coach and Commitment

Husbands, in the same way be considerate as you live with your wives, and treat them with respect as the weaker partner and as heirs with you of the gracious gift of life, so that nothing will hinder your prayers.

(verse 7)

THE COMMITMENT required of an Olympic athlete in extra time and effort is well-documented. Those who have played on great teams will recall the commitment that success required. In the spiritual realm, men have also made great commitments. John Wesley, for example, traveled 250,000 miles in 40 years, preached 40,000 sermons, produced 400 books and knew 10 languages. At the age of 83 he was annoyed that he couldn't write more than 15 hours a day without hurting his eyes. At age 86, he was ashamed he could not preach more than twice a day. He complained in his diary that he had an increasing tendency to lie in bed until 5:30 a.m.

A good marriage requires a great commitment. It is, in fact, "until death do you part." As in any unit, there must be one "head coach." One must be the leader or you have a "two-headed monster." Two leaders create disorder. The husband is given the leadership position in marriage (Ephesians 5:23). But the best leader must be so committed that he encourages loyalty and love in the follower. The wife is given to help the husband. She is a part of him. He is to love and protect her as he would love and protect himself. He is to be willing to die, if need be, for her safety (Ephesians 5:25).

Woman is weaker physically and emotionally. This does not mean women are intellectually inferior. Deep inside, a woman wants to be a woman and treated like a woman, just as a man wants to be manly and treated like a man. For this reason, the "women's liberation" movement is doomed. When women step out of their role to become "liberated," they don't go upward but downward! Their rightful position is one of honor and respect in the family. While the wife must recognize her weakness and look accordingly to her husband for protection, the husband must be considerate of her and treat her as someone special. A good leader never talks down to those under his authority and a good husband never talks down to his wife. Rather, he will try to build her up and encourage her to her highest level of achievement.

The result of good leadership is harmony in the home. When there is harmony at home, prayer — the key to strength for living — is not hindered. But when there is dishonoring, there is no prayer. Effective prayer occurs only without anger or disputing (1 Timothy 2:8).

Husband, how committed to your wife are you? Does your commitment and consideration to your wife match your commitment to your job? If so, you should find harmony and peace at home.

RIGHTEOUS RELATIONSHIPS

1. The husband is the head of the wife.
2. Men and women differ physically and emotionally.
3. The husband is to be committed to his wife.
4. The husband is to be especially considerate and respectful of his wife.
5. Disharmony hinders prayer to God.

---

1 Peter 3:8—16

Repaying Evil with Good

Do not repay evil for evil or insult with insult, but with blessing, because for this you were called so that you may inherit a blessing.

(verse 9)

MANY BASEBALL managers have a policy of retaliation if the opposition knocks down one of their good hitters. They order their own pitchers to pick out an equally good hitter on the other team and to hit him with a pitch! Beanball wars have resulted from such policies.

The Bible makes it clear that retaliation is not God's will. Christians are commanded to repay evil with good. What a different response from the world's ways! The inevitable natural reaction of a pagan society which has tried to eliminate God is to persecute Christians. We promote the terrible abomination of homosexuality and murder innocent newborn babies by the millions. We have tried to ban prayer and the reading of God's Word in public schools, which were originally established for the purpose of teaching people to read and to understand Scripture. We have tried to explain away His role in creation by the absurd notion of evolution. As in Peter's day, a more severe persecution cannot be far away unless there is a turning to God and a forsaking of sin in America.

66

There will be unfair treatment. There will be slander. There should not be, but there will be. If we refused to respond to mistreatment by striking back, it would stop all the fighting and cliques in an organization — a team, a class, a church. We must commit the offender to the Lord and let Him handle him. When criticized, we must turn away from evil, deceitful speech. We are not to become passive, but to actively pursue peace and the good of others (verse 11).

How can we do this? We can do it because we know God hears the prayers of the righteous. We can cry out to God for help, for He has promised to hear us (verse 12). He has not promised to hear the prayer of a sinner — except when he cries out for forgiveness and for the Lord Jesus to be his Savior. The idea that a wicked man can cry out for help in a sticky situation and be heard by God is unscriptural. Only when that man repents and gets right with God through Jesus Christ is God committed to hear and answer his prayer for help. But God is committed to hearing the prayer of a righteous man who has trusted Christ. Make no mistake — We will suffer in this life. Pliny described how early Christians were curtly told, "curse Christ or die." Many turned from following Jesus at this point. But we ought not to fear man (verse 14). When we suffer for righteousness sake, we should remember to fear only God. We are blessed to suffer for Him.

How can we obtain grace to live this way? How can we be always ready to give a reason for our eternal hope (verse 15)? By studying the Word of God. Tragically, so few Christians really know God's Word. Do you have a little chapel in your heart where Jesus is enthroned and peace reigns? All believers need one, and the knowledge of God's Word will help keep that peace.

Another way we suffer unjustly is via the gossip of people. If our conscience is clear, we won't have to spend time refuting all the rumors of gossips, because we'll know they are untrue (verse 16).

Good behavior is the best defense against unjust suffering. And it is the only one God blesses.

1. In what ways have you been treated unjustly?
2. How do you react when treated unfairly?
3. What are the prospects for unfair treatment in the future?

---

1 Peter 3:17—22

When Suffering Is God's Will

It is better, if it is God's will, to suffer for doing good than for evil.

(verse 17)

WHEN GENERAL "STONEWALL" JACKSON lost an arm in battle, his chaplain exclaimed, "Oh, General, what a calamity!" Jackson thanked him for his sympathy, but replied, "You see me wounded, but not depressed, not unhappy. I believe it has been according to God's holy will, and I acquiesce entirely in it. You may think it strange, but you never saw me more perfectly contented than I am today, for I am sure my heavenly Father designs this affliction for my good. I am perfectly satisfied that either in this life or in that which is to come, I shall discover that what is now regarded a calamity is a blessing."

As human beings, we were created for perfection. We had a perfect environment. But sin entered the picture and fouled everything. We remain idealistic and perfectionistic, but the reality is that there is suffering in this world. We'd like to avoid suffering, but it is inevitably par for the course in this sinful world. Despite the heresy that we can have unlimited health, wealth, and prosperity and have it all now, the fact is that sometimes (not always) suffering is part of God's will. False accusations by evil men were aimed at Jesus and His apostles and we can expect no less. The most conscientious Christian will not escape slander. All experience disappointment, loss, and physical pain. Peter tells those who suffer according to God's will to simply commit themselves to their faithful Creator and continue to do good (4:19). Doing good seems to be the theme of a right response to suffering (2:15, 20).

Once again, Jesus is our example. He suffered unfairly, but according to God's will. The Spirit of Christ was in Noah, an Old Testament prophet (1:11), and Jesus preached to rebellious men through Noah as he built the ark long ago. Both the Spirit of Christ and Noah suffered unjust ridicule in those days. But as a result, Noah and his family were saved and given a clear conscience before God. The small number of people (eight total) who were saved in the ark is an encouragement to the "little flock" in Asia and to Christians who are in the minority today.

For the sake of making one's stance public and bold before men in spite of persecution, Peter encourages believers to be baptized. This public act would save them from the temptation to sacrifice a good conscience before God to avoid persecution. They would be clearly identified with Jesus. We would say they "came out of the closet."

What is your response to unjust suffering? Do you continue to do good? Are you bold in your stance for Christ? If not, you can begin now!

RIGHTEOUS RELATIONSHIPS

1. Suffering is to be expected in this life.
2. Suffering is sometimes (not always) God's will.
3. Doing good is the right response to suffering.
4. We long for perfection because we were made for it.
5. Baptism is a bold step which gives us the power of a good conscience towards God.

69

GOD'S WOMAN
IN THE COACHING PROFESSION

FEMALE COACHES have a particularly tough job in the 1990s. So many issues are part of their lives, it is mind-boggling. Traditional standards and role expectations are under attack. Satan has already established a beach head in America in relation to male/female relationships and it is pure spiritual warfare to reclaim lost ground. Following are several potential areas of conflict for the female coach. The Scripture references will be most helpful in giving guidance for each area.

Singleness and Dating

It is not true that everyone needs to be married to live a fulfilled life. The Apostle Paul never married (so far as we know). He felt he could devote more time and energy to the Lord and His work by staying single (See 1 Corinthians 7). Certainly there is more time to devote to players on a team if one has no family to come home to each evening.

But deep in the heart of most women (and men) is the God-given desire to marry and have a family. Genesis 2:18 says it is not good to be alone. If that is true with you, what kind of man do you want to marry? It is good to list your criteria before you even accept a date, for every date should be viewed as a possible marriage partner. I challenge you to list your goals and criteria in this area right now!

If you date, you'll need to make many decisions regarding priorities. Before marriage, your dating relationship can be a lower priority. Once you marry, only your relationship with God is more important! If you are a Christian, only another Christian is a valid dating partner. And he won't be found in bars or at wild parties!

You probably know that God's rules for a healthy relationship prohibit *any* sexual contact outside of marriage (1 Corinthians 6:18—20, 1 Thessalonians 4:3—8). Be careful not to defraud your date by dress, innuendo, or circumstances. Expect the same from him. (To defraud means to raise passions that you cannot *righteously* satisfy.) If God expects you to hold high standards in a terribly permissive era, He will give you the power to live that way (1 Corinthians 10:13). Are you debating whether to do or not to do something on a date? *Decide before you go out!* Use the following questions to give you insight:

1. Will it bring glory to God? (1 Corinthians 10:31)
2. Will it harm my body? (1 Corinthians 6:18, 19)
3. Will it harm my testimony? (Matthew 5:13—16)
4. Is it a stumbling block to others? (1 Corinthians 8:9)
5. Is it a weight in my life? (Hebrews 12:1)
6. Can we do it in Jesus' name? (Colossians 3:17—23)
7. Can we pray for God's guidance? (Proverbs 10:22)
8. Does it seem wrong or have a bad name?
   (1 Thessalonians 5:21, 22)
9. Is it of the world? (1 John 2:15—17)
10. Would I be ashamed to tell my parents about it?
11. Would I feel comfortable doing it if Christ were (physically) beside me?

These questions are effective in any area, but especially in dating. A final note: You don't "fall in love." If you fell into it, it's a *trap!* Love is a decision, not an *emotion.* Love is when you make up your mind to keep a commitment, regardless. Decisions based on emotions rather than commitment will only lead to "self-inflicted" difficulties.

Marriage and the Wife's Role

Just as there are basic roles to be played on any athletic team, there are different roles to be played by men and women for the good of both in society. While Scripture has little to say about a woman's role in government and in industry, it has much to say about her role in marriage and in the church. Contrary to the opinions of many today, God has created the sexes with basic differences and given them different responsibilities. Neither is inferior or superior. Each needs the other. Let's examine some of the many differences between the sexes and the implications for their functions in a man-woman relationship.

Neurologists have discovered that certain areas of the brain control specific behaviors. Women are generally more person-oriented, with earlier development of verbal and social skills than males (a left-brain function). Men have superior visual-spatial skills and can manipulate three-dimensional objects in their minds more easily (a right-brain function). Men are more acclimated to a world of things. Women are equipped to contribute a more personal touch to this impersonal world of things.

Physically, the average adult male is larger and stronger because of the male hormone (testosterone). The average female has a higher percentage of body fat (15% to 27%), a smaller bone and muscle mass, a smaller heart, less aerobic capacity (endurance), and a wider hip girth to facilitate childbirth. Differing joint structures make many young girls more flexible than boys.

Emotionally, the female is affected by monthly changes in her body. Pre-menstrual syndrome (PMS) can cause one to quickly become emotional. Irritability, a quick temper, and poor sportsmanship often flare out of control during the menstrual cycle.

Sexually, males tend to be aroused by sight (suggestive clothes, etc.) and females by touch — facts with obvious implications for hazards in dating relationships.

The point is this: today's idea of "unisex" is ungodly. Our Heavenly Father made the sexes distinct from one another, that each might compliment the other. Men should assume their God-given roles as providers and protectors, honoring women as the weaker partner (1 Peter 3:7). Wives should find fulfillment in the role of helper and encourager, submitting to their husbands (Ephesians 5:22). In so doing, both find God's ideas on the subject are the best ideas.

Before a girl says, "I do," she must be certain she can be loyal, submissive and obedient to her future husband. (If she cannot, the marriage should not take place, for it most likely will not last. While each is equal in value to God (Galatians 3:28), the wife is to be subject to the husband for two reasons. She is subject because Adam was created first. Also, she is subject because it was Eve that was deceived (1 Timothy 2:11—15). Adam, the head of the human race, *knowingly disobeyed* God and is responsible for the consequences. Eve was *deceived* by Satan.

A godly wife finds much joy in supporting her husband (1 Timothy 2). The call of God to being a wife and mother is a high calling. In fact, there is none higher. It is to be more important than a woman's career — or she should not marry in the first place. While working outside the home is not prohibited in Scripture, there are many possible dangers. The working wife often gives many of her best hours to another authority. She is pressured to neglect her first calling as wife and mother, and may become competitive in marriage. It becomes a temptation to reverse her God-appointed role with that of her husband. Her loyalties can easily become divided.

The subordinate role is really the easiest to fulfill! While the head coach makes the decisions (with counsel from the subordinate), *he* is responsible. If they fail, he takes the heat! That's why a godly man listens to the input of a godly wife. He knows he needs all of her support and wise counsel.

God's Woman and Coaching

Though a woman's ministry to a man is usually limited to marriage, the female coach has a great opportunity to encourage, guide, and influence young girls on her athletic team. She has the chance to train each one to be godly in every relationship. That's why it is important for the coach to be walking with God herself. *You can't give what you haven't got!*

A proper view of athletics is important. *The value of athletics depends upon how they are coached.* Many single female coaches are tempted to become "power hungry" in the name of women's rights. Their bitterness takes the fun out of the game for the girls and adversely affects their identity. If a coach handles the girls under her properly, they will be led to demonstrate attitudes of discipline, tolerance, respect, fair play, and leadership. Balance is crucial in women's athletics, for girls must play aggressively without developing a brash hardness with an ungodly attitude. A contrite spirit honors God and He will honor it in return. But arrogance and pride He will not honor. He "stiff-arms" the proud. Team Bible Studies, FCA meetings, and individual counseling from God's Word can help girls to understand the lady-like qualities God wants to develop in their character.

God's Woman and Friendships

All of us need encouragement and support. For the unmarried female coach, the loneliness, long hours, and pressures to win can trap her into an emotional attachment she really does not want or need. The question is, "Who do you really rely on?" Is it the Lord Jesus Christ? He alone can give you the support you need.

It's great to have several good friends instead of only one close friend of the same sex. We become less "co-dependent" upon others when we have many friends. When the emotional ties become strong, the temptation to sexual intimacy, even with another woman, is stronger. Homosexuality and lesbianism have become common. Romans 1:26 warns that, "God gave them over to shameful lusts. Even their women exchanged natural relations for unnatural ones." It is a terrible thing to be "given over" by God. That level of depravity is a tough road and it's a long way back to God. Only through repentance and a consistent walk with God can He heal the hurt it causes. The battle begins in the mind. If desire for physical pleasure overcomes the will to follow Jesus, the war is lost. Christian friends, Bible study, and prayer will keep you from becoming a slave to this sin.

Example

I'd rather see a sermon than to her one any day;
I'd rather one should walk with me than merely show
    the way;
The eye's a better pupil and more willing than the ear;
Fine counsel is confusing, but examples are always clear.

And best of all the preachers are the men who live
    their creeds;
For to see good put into action is what everybody needs.
I soon can learn to do it, if you'll let me see it done;
I can see your hands in action, but your tongue too fast
    may run.

And the lectures you deliver may be very fine and true,
But I'd rather get my lesson by observing what you do;
For I may misunderstand you and the high advice you give;
But there's no misunderstanding how you act and how
    you live.

— Author Unknown

Role Relationships

Dear Father,

I recognize that Satan has used a bitter spirit in many lives to disrupt the unity of God's Spirit. Today I am asking You to forgive me for my bitterness toward any other member — male or female — of Christ's body or outside of His body. Thank You for the diversity of Your church. Forgive us for our criticism of one another.

I ask that You give me a spirit of love, joy and peace as I coach the players on my team. Make me an example of Your patience and concern for others. Give me a gentle spirit and help me to find great joy in the role You have given me in dating, marriage and coaching. Lead me not into temptation. Help me to flee all temptations immediately.

Help me to lead in strength while I submit to the authority of those You have placed over me. Thank You for the freedom that comes from relaxing under authority. Thank you that You do not hold me accountable for areas where You have not given me responsibility, but only for my attitude.

May I live my Christian life in such a manner that one day You will be able to say, "Well done, good and faithful servant."

In the Name of Jesus, Amen.,

V. Attitude in Adversity

CONFLICT IS inevitable if you will live for Christ in this evil world system. Let us contend without being contentious in our relationships.

1 Peter 4

Going Against the Grain (verses 1—6) • **79**
Love — Just Do It! (verses 7—11) • **80**
Praise in Suffering (verses 12—19) • **82**

☆ ☆ ☆ ☆ ☆ ☆
Coaching Clinic: Physical Fitness
☆ ☆ ☆ ☆ ☆ ☆

God Hath Not Promised • **85**
Praising God by Conditioning
          His Temple • **86**
Prayer: Adversity • **89**

Going Against the Grain

They think it strange that you do not plunge with them into the same flood of dissipation, and they heap abuse on you.

(verse 4)

WHILE RECOVERING from a knee operation in 1988, Gary Gaetti of the Minnesota Twins trusted Christ as His Savior. He was delivered from excessive drinking into the wee hours, smoking two packs of cigarettes a day and swearing with almost every sentence. "According to His Word," Gaetti told *Sports Illustrated,* "I was living pretty much full speed for the devil. And I guess I was changed drastically, more so than a lot of other people."

Though he played with the same intensity on the field, Gaetti was the target of some criticism. Some writers questioned whether the change in Gary was good for team chemistry. Kent Hrbek, his best friend with whom he used to tour the bars on the road, said, "He's Gary Gaetti on the field — he still has heart and guts and power. But he's somebody I don't know off the field. It's almost like he passed away."

It's not unusual for a man's friends to turn away from him when he becomes a Christian. He *has* become a new person and the very presence of Jesus Christ in his life makes those indulging in sin very uncomfortable. Because the whole direction of our lives has changed, we face ostracism and sometimes outright abuse. Peter tells us to "arm ourselves" to suffer in this way (verse 1). The evil world hated Jesus (John 15:18) and we can be sure it will hate those who follow Him closely.

When a person lives for Christ, he may not be invited to certain functions related to his profession. He may be passed over for career promotions. He may be discounted as not being competitive or proficient. Even though the unsaved reap many benefits from the goodness and love of the Lord's people, they still slander them!

Sometimes the slights and abuses hurt. But we are answerable to God, not to man. When we were unsaved, we brought no glory to God and caused ourselves many problems. We hate to think of the way we wasted our past. The scorn of man is well worth a wonderful new life in Christ!

Life is short. Time passes quickly. Judgment day will vindicate us. We will look back on today's suffering and it will seem so insignificant. Let us live for Christ now, regardless of the opinions of others.

ATTITUDE IN ADVERSITY

1. We must be prepared to suffer because of loving Jesus.
2. We are much better off as believers than we were as unsaved men.
3. God will vindicate us one day.
4. We live unto God by His Spirit.

---

1 Peter 4:7—11

Love — Just Do It!

Above all, love each other deeply, because love covers over a multitude of sins.

(verse 8)

JACKIE ROBINSON was a courageous man as well as a great athlete. He is remembered for becoming the first black man to play in the major leagues. The year was 1947, and Jackie had to endure much verbal and physical abuse from both fans and players. One day, when he reacted to a dirty player who intentionally drove his spikes into Jackie's chest on a play at second base, the crowd howled at him in rage, calling him names and throwing trash. Shortstop Pee Wee Reese called time out, walked over to his teammate, and put his arm around him in a great show of support. This courageous act demonstrated a love that helped Jackie through a rough time in his life.

Peter tells us that we are near the end of all things. Present world conditions underline this fact. Therefore, any suffering we endure now will be short. Only those things that will last for eternity are worth the investment now. Loving concern for others, as Pee Wee Reese demonstrated to Jackie Robinson, is of great value. As the popular commercial says, "Just do it!" Too often Christians waste their time bickering over minor points of doctrine. We forget we are teammates in an evil world system manipulated by an evil devil. We must remain clear-minded and self-disciplined so we can pray distinctly in times of trial. Therefore, we have little time for the filth poured out via the world's media.

Surface "back slapping" can be so shallow that it gets in the way of real relationships. When Peter says to love each other "deeply," he is using the Greek word (ektené) which describes the taut muscles of an athlete straining to win a race. It means "stretched" or "strained." We must "strain" ourselves to maintain love for other believers in all circumstances. We are not blind to faults, but loving in spite of them. We overlook the sins that others commit against us, even if they don't realize what they did!

Peter next writes about serving others. While we can serve without loving, we cannot love others without serving them. God has given us all various gifts to be used to serve others. Each gift demonstrates God's grace and draws others to the Savior. Hospitality is one gift of God which would have been vital in the days when Christians were driven from their homes and needed food and shelter. Speaking for God is a gift, and it may be done with confidence after much prayer and study of God's Word. Whenever, we love and serve others, whether in a show of friendship, in counseling them about a problem, in giving a sports clinic, or in helping them with food or shelter, it must be done as unto the Lord (Colossians 3:23). He deserves the praise, glory and power forever!

ATTITUDE IN ADVERSITY

1. We must lovingly serve others.
2. We are to "stretch" ourselves to love and serve.
3. We must do everything as unto the Lord.
4. God deserves the praise and glory for every deed.

---

1 Peter 4:12—19

Praise in Suffering

Dear friends, do not be surprised at the painful trial you are suffering, as though something strange were happening to you. But rejoice that you participate in the sufferings of Christ, so that you may be overjoyed when his glory is revealed.

(verses 12, 13)

WASHINGTON REDSKIN coach Joe Gibbs has walked with God through many years of good times and bad. In 1988, he was presented the Tom Landry award to recognize his commitment to physical and spiritual excellence. At that time, he stated that there are two ways to confront adversities. "I realize that if you just commit your life to Christ, to God, and put Him first, everything will fall into place," he said. "As a coach . . . I see people in a matter of two weeks go from hero to bum. There is God's view of life and the world's view. Don't get caught up in the world's view. The world tells you . . . power, position, and money. God says, put me first, and all the other things I will give you."

The Christians to whom Peter wrote had to maintain this same perspective in suffering. The maniacal Roman despot Nero had burned his own city and blamed the believers for it. He covered many with pitch and lit them afire to light his imperial gardens at night. Anticipating that provincial officials might follow Nero's lead, Peter wrote to believers scattered around the empire to prepare them for tough times ahead. His letter seems so relevant to believers in the 1990s.

Trials are painful, but not a strange occurrence in the lives of 20th-century Christians. We can expect them to increase in a world hostile to Jesus and His gospel. Sometimes there is outward disdain shown to Christian coaches, as to the baseball coach who was forbidden by administrators to use his Christian philosophy of discipline and decision-making at his state university job. Sometimes it is secret and silent jealousy and hatred by the world because of God's peace in the life of a Christian. Maybe the hardest to endure is the hurt caused by other "Christians" who are not glorifying to God. Many have no motive to share Jesus and look upon us as fanatics when we do. We should walk away from the insult , even though we hurt inside.

God knows about our suffering. The angels know. And Satan and his demons know. We can glorify God before these created intelligences by the way we allow His grace to carry us through the suffering. We must *rejoice* when participating in Jesus' sufferings, realizing that when we suffer for our commitment to Christ, it is really the world hating Him through us.

Let us be careful that it is not for our own sins that we suffer. As Matthew Henry says, "It is not the suffering, but the cause, that makes the martyr." Even God's best servants need so much more maturity that a loving God will correct and punish them on earth. Judgment begins with Christians! We see it throughout America today. God is purifying His people. Hebrews 12:7 says , "Endure hardship as discipline. God is treating you as sons." While on earth, we suffer the worst we will ever suffer and it is temporary. The ungodly, however, are in the best condition now that they'll ever see. Great suffering forever awaits them because they reject Jesus Christ.

We shouldn't be surprised that the world hates us, for it hates Christ. If we aren't hated by some sinners, we're probably not living for Christ. Faithful endurance of suffering is the greatest proof you belong to Him. Vernon McGee says, "If you are being carried around on a silver platter with a silver spoon in your mouth, you must not be God's child, because that is not the way He does things."

God has great purpose in all our suffering. Because a sovereign God causes or allows every trial, we can rejoice in the knowledge that we are gaining ground every day. Jesus is exalted and we become stronger through it all.

When the war with Iraq erupted, an Israeli mother was asked what affect the constant skud missile attacks would have on her young children. "I think it will make them stronger," she replied. That's what suffering does for us. Therefore, we can rejoice in every trial.

ATTITUDE IN ADVERSITY

1. Christians are hated by the world because it hates Christ.
2. Suffering does not mean we are out of God's will. Often it means we are within God's will.
3. God, the angels, and Satan know about all our inner hurts.
4. A sovereign God causes or allows all suffering for a higher purpose.
5. Suffering only strengthens us.
6. We obey God when we rejoice that we suffer for Jesus.

GOD HATH NOT PROMISED

God hath not promised skies always blue,
    Flower-strewn pathways all our lives through;
God hath not promised sun without rain,
    Joy without sorrow, peace without pain.

God hath not promised we shall not know
    Toil and temptation, trouble and woe;
He hath not told us we shall not bear
    Many a burden, many a care.

God hath not promised smooth roads and wide,
    Swift, easy travel, needing no guide;
Never a mountain, rocky and steep,
    Never a river, turbid and deep.

But God hath promised strength for the day,
    Rest for the laborer, light for the way,
Grace for the trials, help from above,
    Unfailing sympathy, undying love.

— Annie Johnson Flint

PRAISING GOD BY
CONDITIONING HIS TEMPLE

WHEN THE PEOPLE of God built His temple during the reign of Solomon, it was under the specific direction of the Creator Himself. The pre-cut foundation stones fit perfectly and the inner walls were paneled with cedar and overlaid in gold. The glory of God came down and indwelt this wonder of the ancient world!

Today God does not dwell in temples made with human hands (Acts 17:24). Rather, He indwells the physical body of those who trust His Son, the Lord Jesus Christ as their personal Savior. Phenomenal! When you received Jesus, the Spirit of the God of this universe indwelt this body!

Do you not know that your body is a temple of the Holy Spirit, who is in you, whom you have received from God? You are not your own; you were bought at a price. Therefore honor God with your body.

1 Corinthians 6:19, 20

Since we do not own this physical body, we must be sure it is kept in the best condition for our Master's use. Among other things, this means that regular physical exercise is part of the spiritual worship due our Creator (Romans 12:1). Optimal frequency, intensity and duration varies for each individual and it is our responsibility to discover that which is best for our height, weight, and age. Spiritual discipline is then required to maintain physical fitness. Some wrongly believe that physical condition can be neglected while everything is okay "spiritually." But is uncontrolled eating really any less a sin than drunkenness? Or adultery? Or stealing? Certainly, all sins are ugly in God's sight.

Approximately thirty physiological reasons why physical conditioning is beneficial to God's temple could be listed. Suffice it to say that the heart and respiratory system become more efficient (laboring less to do the same amount of work), undesirable fat deposits in the blood and other areas of the body are eliminated, protective proteins in blood are increased, and the body becomes more resistant to disease and stress. Needless to say, the conditioned individual feels better, has less sickness, looks better, and has more endurance to meet his daily demands. How many coaches have not become all that God wanted them to be because of unfaithful stewardship of the physical body?

As a steward of the grace of God, are you convinced you must condition God's temple? Do you know you must condition yourself also in consideration of others? Obesity can be a stumbling block to someone with whom you may want to share the gospel. An undisciplined lifestyle may hinder someone else from finding the Savior. Do you think Jesus was overweight? Of course not! Then why should any of His servants be obese?

Are you married? Husbands, your body belongs to your wife (1 Corinthians 7:4, 5). You are grossly inconsiderate of her if you do nothing about an overweight problem. Wives, did you know your mate is primarily stimulated visually? You may be ruining your sexual relationship with your own husband. When that happens, marriage problems are inevitable.

God considers the body of a believer to be very important:

Don't you know that you yourselves are God's temple and that God's Spirit lives in you? If anyone destroys God's temple, God will destroy him; for God's temple is sacred, and you are that temple.
1 Corinthians 3:16, 17

There is nothing evil about the physical body! Though we suffer because the effects of sin have caused weakness, the body itself is not evil. It's easy to see why many people who believe the body to be evil have severe self image problems! Our bodies were created by God as a temple for His Spirit. He made each of us in unique fashion. We should thank and praise Him for His wisdom in their design and glorify Him by maintaining them to the maximum.

Someone says, "bodily exercise profits little" (1 Timothy 4:8). That's true, but we should want all the profit available for the glory of God! Many coaches deny their responsibility toward God's temple by quoting this verse because they really don't want to discipline themselves. As children of the Living God, we are to love and care for our bodies (Ephesians 5:28, 29). Discipline in physical exercise is indispensable.

The human body was designed by God for motion. (Even for those who are not obese, a sedentary lifestyle is contrary to what is best for health. Our example in physical fitness, as in every area, is the Lord Jesus Himself. Though He could have ridden up and down Palestine on the best Arabian horse, He walked everywhere He went. Only once is it recorded that He rode, and that was on a donkey when He went into Jerusalem. Jesus not only worked physically as a carpenter when growing up, but He also remained a physically active person until He died on the cross for your sins and mine.

So let's go, coach! If it's been years since you've exercised, consult your doctor for a physical examination. Then begin a regular fitness program and stay with it!

Adversity

Dear Father,

I come to You in the wonderful name of the Lord Jesus Christ, by whom You made the universe. I acknowledge Him as creator of the bodies of man, beginning with Adam in the Garden of Eden. It was Your delight to create us and it is by Your wisdom that we function. We do not understand all your miraculous ways and means, but we worship and hallow You for who You are and for giving us life.

Father, I realize that in everything You work for our good. Even the bad things like sickness and loss can be turned for Your glory. But at the same time, we do not seek pain and suffering. We hurt and have players who hurt. In some cases we sense a spiritual attack from the enemy. I have totally given you my body, my life, and this athletic program. You have given influence and athletes have learned of Jesus because of Your work through me in this job. Now, Satan has come to steal, to kill and to destroy. He has attacked our health in various ways.

Father, You said when the enemy comes in like a flood the Spirit of the Lord would lift up a standard against him to put him to flight. Since You said whatever is bound on earth is bound in heaven, I declare every attacking spirit of frustration, sickness and criticism to be bound concerning this program.

To Satan I say: This is God's program and you have no business here. I resist you in Jesus' name, you roaring but toothless lion, and command you to flee from me and from this work. The Lord rebuke you!

Father, since our Lord Jesus is still the Great Physician, I ask you to step in and remove frustration from the players, still the criticism of teammates, and heal injuries and illnesses on the team. May each player be aware that it is You who did this and give You glory. Thank you for the opportunity to coach and for the opportunity to play these games. May your holy will be done in each life and may each circumstance point more players to our Living Lord Jesus.

In Jesus' Name, Amen.

VI. To Every Head Coach

THOUGH GEORGE McINTYRE led his team to the Hall of Fame Bowl in 1984, he had a losing record during seven seasons at Vanderbilt University. Yet, he was a winner in the things that last. Coach Mac now leads with the same values at a high school in Nashville, Tennessee.

1 Peter 5

Lead by Example (verses 1—4) • **92**
Lead with Humility (verses 5—7) • **94**
Lead Against the Enemy (verses 8, 9) • **96**
The Temporary Nature of Suffering
    (verses 10—14) • **97**

☆ ☆ ☆ ☆ ☆ ☆
Coaching Clinic: Leadership
☆ ☆ ☆ ☆ ☆ ☆

Leadership and Team Cohesion • **100**
Characteristics of Leadership • **103**
Developing Leadership in Team Captains • **106**
Chain of Command • **108**
The Assistant Coach and His Effectiveness • **109**
Prayer: Team Morale • **111**

Lead by Example

. . . not lording it over those entrusted to you, but being examples . . .

(verse 3)

JACK GRONT has been called the teacher who shaped a legend. In the summer of 1950, he became the club pro at a course in Columbus, Ohio. It was there that Jack Nicklaus' father introduced him to his young son. Gront instilled three fundamentals in young Nicklaus. He encouraged him to extend his swing arc as far as possible, which possibly led to his famous flying right elbow. He taught him to stand flatfooted, but to lift the left heel on the swing — another Nicklaus trademark. Finally, he made Jack keep his head absolutely still. Nicklaus preaches the same basics today, even to the point of holding on to the hair of his sons' heads to keep them still, just as Gront did to his!

The influence and example of a coach is tremendous — even more so than we realize. Jack Nicklaus never realized the effect Jack Gront would have on his life. Our leadership and example is crucial to the development of young lives. Peter gives some great advice to leaders during times of suffering in Chapter 5 of his letter. Let's listen in on his "coaching clinic."

As a leader, Peter is qualified to write to leaders. He encourages leaders (elders) to set the example for God's people. There are many people with titles of "leader" or "coach" today, but we have a crisis in leadership! The leader is to set the pace and encourage others to follow, not because someone forces him to lead, but because he wants to lead. There is no place for reluctant leadership today.

Money must not be his motive in leading. In fact, material riches are not conducive to character development. As church leaders must feed, not "fleece" the flock, coaches must work with players for the *benefit* of the kids and not to their detriment. The coach who coaches for the money is not the most effective. Power over others must not be the motive. Some coaches are on a tremendous ego trip and get their kicks out of ordering others around. Power is also the wrong motive in leading (coaching).

The best motive for leadership is to serve others. We must see our leadership role as directing people because they need direction. Tom Landry once defined coaching as "making people do what they don't want to do to achieve what they want to achieve." Coaching is a serving role in this sense. This is entirely contrary to the world's method of domination over the lives of others. We are to lead by example. People will follow one who "practices what he preaches."

There is another motive for leadership. Jesus Christ, our "Chief Shepherd" (leader) will reward good leadership with a crown of glory some day! We are not working for nothing! We are to be given *eternal* rewards. The world's honors, its inflated salaries, and its ego-building power over others are nothing compared to the eternal crown of glory Jesus will one day give to faithful leaders of His people. There is a bright future for faithful, godly leaders.

TO EVERY HEAD COACH

1. A good leader must be an example of good character.
2. A leader must not be reluctant.
3. Serving others must be the motive in leading them.
4. A good leader uses power to benefit those who follow him.
5. Jesus will reward faithful leaders some day.

Lead with Humility

Young men, in the same way, be submissive to those who are older. All of you, clothe yourselves with humility toward one another, because, "God opposes the proud but gives grace to the humble. Humble yourselves, therefore under God's mighty hand that he may lift you up in due time. Cast all your anxiety on him because he cares for you.

(verses 5—7)

HUMILITY AND UNSELFISHNESS were credited with helping the New York Giants to the Super Bowl XXI Championship. Led by quarterback Phil Simms, the Giants polished off the Denver Broncos, 39—20. The methodical Simms set a Super Bowl accuracy record with 22 completions in 25 attempts. "No, I don't feel ignored, " Simms said softly, when asked about the lavish attention given rival quarterback John Elway. "When you think of the Denver Broncos, you think of Elway. When you think of the Giants, you don't think of Simms." Center Bart Oates added, "We don't have stars or egos. Well, we do have stars, but they don't look at themselves like that."

All leaders need a dose of humility and unselfishness similar to that demonstrated by Phil Simms and Bart Oates. No leader knows it all. We all need the counsel and advice of others. Even the President of the United States receives the counsel of others, and in that sense is submissive to them. We must submit to one another if we are to benefit from their advice. The foolish pride of Saddam Hussein refused to submit to others. He lost his military machine and hundreds of thousands of soldiers because of his pride. He executed anyone who disagreed with him! In contrast, Christians are to put on humility like a coat.

There is a mutual antagonism between God and the proud man. God has ways of casting down the proud. When the Bible says, "God opposes the proud," it literally means he "sets Himself against them." He "stiff-arms" proud men and women. As a ball carrier fends off a would-be tackle with a stiff-arm, God keeps proud people away from close fellowship with Himself, while He gives grace to the humble. Pride in self disgusts God. Pastor Don Finto expresses it uniquely. He says there are two jobs in life. One is to be humbled. The second is to be exalted. The first is your job, the second is God's. We are to humble ourselves, and God will exalt us in due time. But if we insist on doing God's job (exalting self), He will do our job (humble us).

Lest we worry about our place in life or our suffering circumstances, Peter tells us to cast *all* our anxiety upon God. Why can we safely trust Him? Because He cares for us. Even the most dedicated Christian coaches sometimes work with anxious care and worry. This worry saps our strength and is very burdensome. It is sinful. But a firm belief in the goodness and the righteousness of a Holy God calms our fearful spirits. He knows us and He cares for us.

TO EVERY HEAD COACH

1. Younger folks are to submit to older people because experience is to be honored.
2. Good leaders need the counsel of others.
3. Receiving good advice requires submission to others.
4. We must humble ourselves and God will lift us up.
5. Because God cares for us, we can cast all our anxiety upon Him.

Lead Against the Enemy

Be self-controlled and alert. Your enemy the devil prowls around like a roaring lion looking for someone to devour. Resist him . . .

(verse 8)

HEAVYWEIGHT CHAMPION Jack Johnson learned to be careful about who he trusted in an October 16, 1909, title fight against "Michigan Assassin" Stanley Ketchel. Secretly, they had agreed not to go for knockouts, but Ketchel saw an opening and floored Johnson. The irate champion rose up, stormed across the ring, and dropped Ketchel with a knockout punch so powerful that some reporters claimed that he later found three teeth embedded in his glove.

There is an evil enemy, Satan, loose in the world today and he cannot be trusted. Some day an angel will grab him, bind him, and throw him into the Abyss where he will be locked up for 1000 years. After a short period, he will be loosed temporarily, recaptured, and thrown into a lake of burning sulfur to be tormented day and night forever (See Revelation 20). The destiny of the devil is not very encouraging for him! And he is not a "happy camper" about it! All he can do is "make hay while the sun shines" for him. He hates God and therefore he hates God's children. He will do anything to trip us, confuse us, cause us to sin, and to deny our Lord Jesus. He is a suave, subtle serpent. He has no horns, pointed tail, or red pajamas, but appears as an angel of light. As we walk the path of life, you can bet he's ahead waiting to jump us at every bend in the road. He would devour us if he could. As starved lions mauled and devoured Christians in the Roman Coliseum, Satan would maul and devour us spiritually by destroying our testimony for Jesus today.

Around the world, other Christians face much suffering. It was so in Peter's day and it is so today. If Corrie Ten Boom could withstand a Nazi death camp, if Joni Earickson Tada can overcome paraplegia with joy in the Lord, and if Nora Lam of *China Cry* could stand up to brutal suffering all in Jesus' name, we can stand, too! But we must be under control at all times, not just off the field, but *on* it too. The spiritual war is no less real *during* a game than it is before and after. Satan would love for us to "blow up" and lose our witness to others.

Remember, Satan is powerless against the cross of Jesus. He hates the thought of his defeat on Golgotha. You see, it was at Calvary that Jesus' blood was shed for us. The Righteous One took our place and paid for our sin, and Satan has no power over all those who rest by faith in the merits of Jesus' blood! All we need do is stand firm in the faith (verse 9). God does the rest!

TO EVERY HEAD COACH

1. We must be self-controlled and alert on and off the field.
2. The enemy never sleeps in his schemes to trip us up.
3. The enemy is powerless against Jesus' blood.
4. We only need to stand alert against his devices.
5. Others *can* and *have* suffered for Jesus. So can we.

---

1 Peter 5:10—14

The Temporary Nature of Suffering

And the God of all grace, who called you to his eternal glory in Christ, after you have suffered a little while, will himself restore you and make you strong, firm and steadfast.

(verse 10)

ONE OF THE GREATEST days in track and field history was May 6, 1954. On that day, Roger Bannister broke a longstanding barrier of barriers — the four-minute mile — in Oxford, England. Bannister recalled the final lap of the race in his autobiography: "I felt that the moment of a lifetime had come. . .The world seemed to stand still, or did not exist. The only reality was the next two hundred yards of track under my feet. . .Those last few seconds seemed never-ending. . .The arms of the world were waiting to receive me if only I reached the tape without slackening my speed. . .I leaped at the tape like a man taking his last spring to save himself from the chasm that threatens to engulf him."

The announcer, Norris McWhirter, who would become world famous as compiler of *The Guinness Book of World Records,* dramatically drew out the announcement: "The time is THREE. . ." The roar of the crowd drowned out the rest of his sentence. Bannister's time of 3:59.4 had shattered a great but temporary barrier, and within to and one-half years nine other runners had done the same!

It seemed a long, hard road to shatter the four-minute mile. Sometimes our suffering seems long, hard, and impossible as well. We feel the days will never end. The trials seem to last forever and we wonder if we'll ever live carefree again. But just as the four-minute mile was a temporary barrier, our suffering here on earth is also temporary! The God of all grace has called us to eternal glory. For the 8th time in his brief letter, Peter reminds us of the glory at the end of the road! Our pain lasts relatively only a "little while." "This too shall pass," wrote Solomon. When the suffering has worked God's purpose into our lives, the Lord Himself will "restore us and make us strong, firm, and steadfast." Like pre-season practice, the regimen is tough, but victory will be sweet! We may not like the trials we are called to endure, but we will like the results they work in us!

We gain a newer, larger perspective of life after having endured suffering. The maturity gained enables us to sympathize with and help others. We base our lives not upon the shifting sands of this life, but upon the rock of God's faithfulness. Looking back, the trials seem brief as we emerge victoriously on the other side.

Christian coach, stand fast in God's power and grace. He was not indifferent to the suffering of Christians in Peter's day, and He is not indifferent to yours today. Your suffering is only temporary. The loss of a game, a season, a friend, a loved one, a job, a financial advantage, or any other disappointment is temporary and will be followed by God's restoration. He promises to make you strong, firm and steadfast. With Jesus, the best is always yet to come.

TO EVERY HEAD COACH

1. We are called to eternal glory.
2. Suffering is only temporary.
3. God has many purposes in our suffering.
4. The best is yet to come!

LEADERSHIP AND TEAM COHESION

ONE OF THE GREATEST fears a coach has is that he will lose his team mentally and emotionally. And probably the greatest satisfaction in coaching comes from putting together a cohesive unit to compete on the field. Because moving together with positive direction is so important, we must study how to better achieve the desired level of team cohesion. Every philosophy has certain presuppositions and the following ideas presuppose (1) that God's Word is authoritative and (2) that it is relevant in interpersonal relationships.

The model below illustrates the relationship between the responsibilities of a head coach, the players response to his leadership, and team cohesion.

Servant Leadership
A Responsibility of the Head Coach

The base of the pyramid is the responsiblity of the head coach. Because Jesus said that the greatest leader is one who serves (Matthew 20:25-28), we conclude that the role of "Servant Leader" is the best role for any head coach. Included in that role are the following:

1. **Knowledge** — A coach must study to constantly gain more insight and knowledge of his players and of his profession. No coach who is ignorant of either his players' needs or his sport deserves the respect of the team.

2. **Character** — We cannot give what we do not have. The value of the athletic experience depends upon how it is coached. The character of the coach determines this value. While players can submit to vulgar and immoral coaches, many cannot respect such behavior and their motivation is hindered. On the other hand, strong moral character in coaches encourages the respect of the team.

3. **Love** — This must be the basis for all we do as coaches. If we really love our team members, they will sense it and will respect and respond positively to us.

4. **Discipline** — The coach must provide firm and fair discipline. Lines must be drawn and enforced because human nature is such that people must sense restraints for their own good as well as for the team good. Rules must be relevant, enforceable and reasonable. Punishment must fit the violation.

5. **Organization** — Intelligent organization is crucial for gaining the respect of the team. The coach best serves the team by advance planning of every phase of the program. Nothing is left to chance. An organization is made strong through wise planning.

The second level is the responsibility of the individual players. They are to respect the coach and his position of authority. A player should have no difficulty respecting the coach as just described. However, some players will not "buy into" the value system of the head coach, no matter how much knowledge, character, love, discipline, and organization he demonstrates. These players should leave the program, for team cohesion is not possible if a player fails to respect and respond to his coach.

As communication of these traits and feelings occurs from coach to players and vice versa, the players' respect for the coach grows and internal leadership increases. Captains are selected from among these leaders. The team internalizes a "goal orientation," as encouraged by the coach. Because there is direction, there is a "motive" in playing, an enthusiasm that is not automatic but is achieved by these character traits in players and coach. Our Lord never promised we'd win championships every year, but the team cohesion made possible by the application of these principles frees everyone to release his maximum potential. And that release brings the greatest satisfaction to the "Servant-Leader."

CHARACTERISTICS OF LEADERSHIP

THERE ARE TWO theories of leadership: one, that leaders are born; the second, that leaders are made. Whichever is true, all must agree that through proper knowledge and experience, leadership can be further refined and developed. To be a good leader takes time, but *never* in our history has the need for qualified leadership been greater. Examine some characteristics of successful leaders:

1. Vision — A leader sees beyond what is, to what can be. In a sense, he refuses merely to accept what the eyes can see.

2. Confidence — not cockiness, but great assurance and positiveness of who he is, what he is, and where he is going.

3. Tenacity — A mark of a leader is that he does not leave a trail of half-finished projects, eagerly begun but abandoned when the going got rough.

4. Enthusiasm —The enthusiastic leader is never dampened by "we tried it before and it didn't work." He gets up and gets going. He doesn't wait around for something good to develop. Instead, he makes things happen.

5. Organization — the key to accomplishment. One who has leadership qualities can readily discern between priority and the less essential. He knows how to start and how to proceed. He has a well-thought-out plan which will lead to success.

6. Vitality — Nothing so inspires confidence as someone who is alive, dynamic, and moving forward. Jesus said, "I am come that ye might have life and that ye might have it more abundantly" (John 10:10).

7. Faith — Faith overcomes obstacles and keeps the vision bright even when circumstances appear dim. A leader worth following possesses genuine, personal faith in Jesus Christ. He looks to God daily for his marching orders.

8. Humility — the willingness of a man to place others and their needs ahead of his own, not promoting his own image but the good of the team.

9. Knowledge — The leader must become a real student of the game to win the confidence f the group.

10. Judgment — a combination of intelligence and common sense to make correct decisions.

11. Emotional stability — the ability to cope with conflict in many forms and act with poise.

12. Decisiveness — the ability and the courage to make correct decisions promptly and to stick with them regardless of the criticism.

13. Responsibility — A leader assumes responsibility for his actions and those of the team.

14. Integrity —Personal honesty and morality are required to gain respect and loyalty. Without these, team spirit is quickly destroyed.

15. Initiative — This implies being a self-starter. A leader doesn't wait for good to happen and then jump on the band wagon. He takes the initiative.

16. Cooperation — Leaders must be successful in working with others, realizing that their goals cannot be attained alone. A leader must work with those in authority over him, those equal in authority, and those under him.

17. Relationships — A leader recognizes that every person on the team is important and spends time and effort helping everyone. He never develops his own little clique. He is empathic, perceptive and a good listener.

18. Loyalty — A leader must be loyal to his team, and he may then expect it to be loyal to him. Loyalty leads to unity and cohesiveness within the team.

19. Single-minded — undivided in attention and loyalty. One thing at a time.

20. Goal-oriented — A good leader has one worthy goal and strives for objectives which lead him towards that goal. He is not swayed from his goal, will not compromise and will not allow divided priorities or opposition to impede him. Rather, he sees stress as opportunity and allows it to make him stronger.

21. Communication — A good leader communicates clearly and often. He never allows problems to fester because of lack of talking them out. He speaks like he means it because he does.

22. Optimistic — No pessimist ever made a great leader. The pessimist sees a difficulty in every opportunity. The optimist sees an opportunity in every difficulty.

23. Sense of Humor — A good leader can laugh at himself. He doesn't walk around with a sour countenance, but is able to see the lighter side of tense situations.

24. Physical fitness — A good leader cares enough about his body and his appearance to maintain both throughout life. In so doing, he is able to better meet the demands placed upon him.

DEVELOPING LEADERSHIP
IN TEAM CAPTAINS

A PLAYER doesn't have to be a captain to be a leader. At the same time, being selected captain does not make one a leader. But one thing is sure: Without leadership from team members, the team is doomed to disappointment. So, how is leadership developed? Sometimes it is innate — that is, a person seems to be born with qualities that draw others after him. But leadership can be encouraged and developed (Proverbs 1:2—5). Following are some reasonable expectations a coach may require of team leaders:

DUTIES OF A CAPTAIN:

1. **Desire to be a Team Leader.**
   a. Demonstrate by team spirit and by hustle.
   b. Exhibit leadership on and off the field.
   c. Learn to lead, not to drive.

2. **Help build and maintain team morale.**
   a. Aid all players to get to practice on time.
   b. Set the correct example yourself.
   c. Encourage your teammates when the going gets tough.
   d. Keep griping to a minimum.
   e. Exhibit confidence in who you are, in your team, and in your coaches.
   f. Show a smile and be relaxed — do not show disgust, sulk, or hang your head — keep your chin up.

3. **Be an Assistant to the Coach.**
   a. Provide input on specific skills that need to be covered in practice.
   b. Make suggestions for improving practice to avoid monotony.
   c. Oversee player equipment so that it is not lost.

4. **Act as Spokesman for the Team.**
   a. Participate in pre-game meetings with coaches and umpires for ground rules.
   b. Bring all pertinent information about the team to the attention of the coach (problem players, etc.).
   c. Talk with players regarding attitudes toward training and grades.
   d. Bring questions to the attention of the coach.

5. **Help control training habits.**
   a. Set the example yourself.
   b. Talk encouragingly about training and help others realize its importance.
   c. Remember: training is a year-round process.
   d. Enforce and check on training of team members — but don't try to be a cop.
   e. Avoid and help others avoid places where training is liable to be broken.

Making captains aware of these expectations is the first step in developing leaders. Positive reinforcement (praise) for responsive leadership goes a long way. Most importantly, be a role model. Players will mirror the attitude of coaches and you can't give what you haven't got! Trust God to make you what He wants you to be and you can trust Him with your team!

CHAIN OF COMMAND

IF CAPTAINS are to exert leadership on a team, if individuals are to be motivated to the maximum, and if team cohesion is to be sustained, the concept of chain of command must be discussed and understood. Below is a model, based upon a plan submitted by Coach Bob Marsh.

ATHLETIC DIRECTOR

HEAD COACH

ASSISTANT COACH   ASSISTANT COACH

STUDENT MANAGER   STUDENT MANAGER

TEAM CAPTAINS

RETURNING VETERANS

ROOKIES

Everyone, including the head coach, derives authority because he is under authority. Anytime one under authority steps out from under his authority, he jeopardizes his own authority! For this reason, coaches must never criticize administration, assistant coaches must be loyal to the head coach, and so on. Each authority must receive input and heed advice from those under him. Team captains have much formal responsibility, but returning veterans have as much informal responsibility to set a positive example for new players. Rookies start at the bottom, but are not to be harassed or "bossed around" by upperclassmen. Remember, the greatest leader is a servant, and all should strive to serve the most.

THE ASSISTANT COACH
AND HIS EFFECTIVENESS

JUST AS THERE ARE separate problems and privileges of head coaches, there are unique challenges each assistant coach must face. A long list of both problems and privileges of assistant coaches could be composed. While some assistants find great fulfillment in their jobs, others remain frustrated. Often, job satisfaction relates to the philosophy of the program as set forth by the head coach. Certainly, he has that right and responsibility. Let's look at a model to understand the dynamics of coaching fulfillment and effectiveness for the assistant coach. The solid lines represent an ideal set of circumstances and the dotted lines represent less than ideal circumstnces.

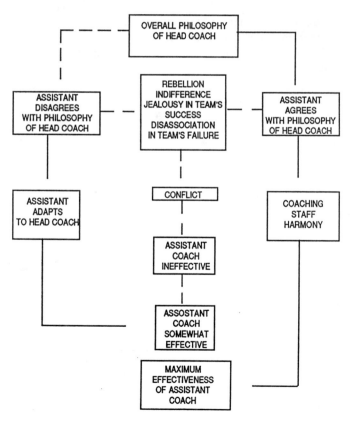

Obviously, assisting a head coach with an identical philosophy and value system is the best situation. Staff harmony and maximal effectiveness is likely to follow, although our old nature can still cause problems. Some assistants become jealous of the head coach and his success and disassociate from his failures. Conflict can result and the resulting ineffectiveness of the assistant can frustate both people. All of us must constantly be on guard against ungodly attitudes.

A less than ideal situation occurs when the assistant has a personal coaching philosophy that differs from the head coach. Rebellion and/or indifference can follow, resulting in conflict and ineffectiveness. However, if the assistant coach submits himself to his superior, understanding that God has put him in his current position for a greater ultimate purpose, God helps him to adapt and he can be effective.

A Sovereign God has different places prepared for His children at different times. Our role is to trust Him in doing the job He has given us until He teaches us the lessons we need to learn. He can be counted upon in the most trying of circumstances.

Team Morale

Father,

I recognize there is a terrible lack of leadership in American culture. It is not the popular thing to step out and show the way to work or to live. Nevertheless, I ask You to make me a strong leader for the cause of Christ and the gospel. I pray that You would ingrain the traits of the Lord Jesus into my life. If that means I need to get more disciplined with players, give me the strength. If it means I need to give more slack to players, please help me. I want to coach as Jesus would have me to coach. Make me a dynamic leader of others for Your glory. May I lead in a Godly direction.

Father, I pray for Your mighty hand to reinforce my leadership on this team. May players sense the authority of the Lord Jesus in my life and may they respond positively to Him. I pray for team leaders to emerge who will stand uncompromisingly for You. Strengthen and bless those who know You on this team. Draw those who don't know You to Yourself with Your loving Holy Spirit. Unify our team for the Glory of God and the good of others.

In the Name of Jesus, Amen.

Second Peter

Faithful Living in Difficult Days

Introduction to Second Peter

LIKE ANY CONCERNED COACH, Peter didn't forget about his men after one season or even after their eligibility had run out. Throughout the rest of his earthly life, he continued to care for the future of the scattered believers. Shortly before he died in 68 a.d. (1:13, 14), he wrote a second letter to stimulate them to wholesome thinking (3:1), to help them combat the coming apostasy (2:1), and to encourage them to grow up in the grace and knowledge of Jesus (3:18). He knew that difficult days were ahead for the people of God. And the knowledge of the Holy One was their only sure defense against the onslaughts of the enemy.

Peter was a great motivator, for he had a rich vocabulary and a public speaker's flare for creative expression. He used many unique words, for of the 686 words that occur only once in Scripture, Peter used 116 of them. His thoughts are brief and to the point, and as we enter the difficult days of the 90s, they are as helpful to us as they were to first century believers. May God use these words to inspire you to faithful living in every trial of life.

VII. Victory in Knowing Jesus

MIKE SCHMIDT was a Hall of Famer on and off the field. As one who knew Jesus Christ, Mike was careful to set a good example of moral character for young people.

2 Peter 1

Knowledge: The Key to Victory (verses 1— 2) • **119**
God's Precious Promises (verses 3—4) • **120**
Character: Make Every Effort to Get It
   (verses 5—11) • **122**
Faith Based Upon Fact (verses 12—21) • **124**

☆ ☆ ☆ ☆ ☆ ☆
Coaching Clinic: Athletics in the 90s
☆ ☆ ☆ ☆ ☆ ☆

The Athlete of the 90s • **127**
Sports and Values in the 90s • **129**
Coaching for Christ in the 90s • **131**
Coaching When the Bottom Falls Out •**132**
Prayer: Seeking God's Coaching Job • **135**

2 Peter 1:1—4

Knowledge: The Key to Victory

Grace and peace be yours in abundance through the knowledge of God and of Jesus our Lord.

(verse 2)

IN 1989, BELGIUM CYCLIST Eric Vanderaerden crossed the finish line of Atlantic City's Tour de Trump finale and wept. For 10 days and 837 miles Vanderaerden had chased the leader of the race and, entering the final stage, trailed by only 50 seconds. But midway through the final day, Vanderaerden missed a right turn, and with no marshal to direct him, followed a motorcycle going the wrong way. He was one-third of a mile off course before doubling back, and he finished 2:34 behind the leader.

"Everything was lost," he said. Asked whether the mistake cost him victory, he replied, "Yes, I think so."

As lack of knowledge cost Eric Vanderaerden a chance of victory, the lack of knowledge of God costs everyone — clergy and laymen alike — in the spiritual realm. When Peter wrote to those who had "received a faith as precious as ours" (verse 1), he was indicating that every layman's faith in Jesus Christ as Savior is no different, no less necessary, equally as privileged, and as great as any preacher's faith. This faith is based upon the *knowledge* of God and of Jesus our Lord. Without this knowledge of Him, we all stumble and miss the turn in the "race of faith."

The knowledge of God is the key to both grace and peace. That knowledge comes through the study of His Word and the revelation of God's Holy Spirit. It comes no other way. God doesn't "zap" us with supernatural dreams and visions to teach us of Himself. He expects us to study His inspired Word.

Daniel wrote that it is the people who know their God who will be able to strongly resist the terrible invasion of Israel during the Great Tribulation (Daniel 11:32). Paul wanted to know Christ and His resurrection power (Philippians 3:10). Peter says that knowledge of Him is the key to receiving His divine power (verse 3).

The first step in knowing God is to trust His Son as Savior. After you *trust* Him, you are ready to get to *know* Him intimately. You will not know God until you put your trust in Him by faith. Will you trust in the Great God and Savior, Jesus Christ? He is trustworthy. He will keep you from many wrong turns in life.

VICTORY IN KNOWING JESUS

1. Knowing Jesus saves you from wrong turns in life.
2. You know Him through His Word and by His Spirit.
3. To know Him, you must first trust Him.
4. One who is not a preacher must know Him as well as one who is a preacher.
5. Knowing God is the key to grace and peace during trials.

---

2 Peter 1:3, 4

God's Precious Promises

Through these he has given us his very great and precious promises . . .

(verse 4)

"IT'S A SAD DAY," said Kansas City Royals General Manager John Schuerholz, in reference to the death of Dick Howser. The 51-year-old former Yankees and Royals manager died of brain cancer in June, 1987. Before his death, Howser had refused to indulge in self-pity.

"We are all going to die," he said the previous winter, "and we don't like it. People are always talking about tomorrow, but there's no guarantee tomorrow will get here. You fight today and hope tomorrow gets better."

We may not be guaranteed of life tomorrow on this earth, but because of God's own glory and goodness, He has made tremendous promises to those who put their faith in His Son. Peter describes these promises as both "very great" and as "precious." They are, in fact, more precious than gold! We have vast riches in the promises of our Heavenly Father.

What are some of God's many promises to His children? Jesus said, "Whoever comes to me I will *never* drive away" (John 6:37). What an invitation to come to the Savior! What assurance of salvation! Paul wrote, "All who are in Christ are *new creations!* We are not what we were, but now possess His divine nature!" (2 Corinthians 5:17). 1 John 5:11—13 promises us *eternal life* in Jesus. We are also promised here that we can *know,* based upon belief in Jesus, that we have eternal life. Because God cannot and would not lie, our future is secure. Verses 14—15 of this passage promise that God hears and answers prayer. In Matthew 11:28—29, Jesus promises us *rest* from the weariness of the world when we come to Him. He promises to be with us always to the very end of the age (Matthew 28:20). He promises us food, clothing and freedom from worry (Matthew 6:25—34). 1 Peter 1:4 promises us an inheritance kept for us in Heaven. When Jesus ascended to Heaven, God sent two angels to promise that He will one day physically return to this earth (Acts 1:10, 11). What a promise! 1 Thessalonians 4:13—18 says that He will come with a shout, the dead in Christ will be resurrected, and living believers will be caught up with them to meet Him and to be forever with Him!

God's promises are very great and precious to His people. They are enough to bring hope to the most discouraged, for He cannot lie. Every promise will be fulfilled in His perfect time.

VICTORY IN KNOWING JESUS

1. God has made great promises to us.
2. They are precious to us as we walk through life.
3. Because He cannot lie, all promises will be fulfilled.

Character:
Make Every Effort to Get It!

For this very reason, make every effort to add to your faith goodness; . . .

(verse 5)

CY YOUNG has a yearly award given in his name to baseball's outstanding pitcher. For more than two decades around the turn of the century, Young was one of the great pitchers in baseball. He had great control, walking just 29 batters in 380 innings during the 1904 season. Cy also had great control as a person. He never argued with umpires, and in an era where graciousness and clean-living among ballplayers was uncommon, his personal character set him apart from the profane. No wonder the Cy Young award is given in his honor.

Because of their faith in Christ, Christians are to exemplify His character at all times. We are to stand out from the world as Cy Young did from the immorality of his day, and we are to "make every effort" to do so. We are to add the traits listed by Peter in ever-increasing amounts (verse 8), for we must grow as any living thing grows. If there is no growth, there must be no life! Decay is the only alternative!

What are the traits we are to add to our lives? Peter lists seven which correspond to those listed by Paul (Galatians 5:22, 23). First, we must add *goodness* to our faith. This trait includes virtue, strength, valor, and excellence in everything we do. This trait alone is in stark contrast to the world around us!

Knowledge is listed second. No premium is placed upon ignorance. We gain knowledge by study of God's Word and through experience. Knowledge of God leads to spiritual power and growth (Colossians 1:9, 10). *Discipline* (self-control) is next to be added. In an increasingly undisciplined society, one who is personally disciplined

122

stands out. We must live with physical, mental, and spiritual discipline at all times. The world, and even many who claim Christianity, often don't want anything to do with self-control (Acts 24:25), but we must have it to live effectively and productively.

Because we are born to trouble, *perseverance* is another necessary trait. We must see beyond current pressures and problems to the ultimate outcome. We must endure under adversity without giving up or giving in to them. Next, we are to add *godliness*. We are to defer to God, desiring to be like Him with a reverent attitude toward Him.

To godliness, we add *brotherly kindness* — a tenderness of heart toward all believers. We are to have care and concern for others instead of a hard heart towards them and their needs.

Finally, we must love others as ourselves. Love is the answer to the problems of the world. God is love and as His followers we cannot ignore His command that we love others.

The Christian walk is a serious course, not an extracurricular activity. Walking the road of life with these character traits is not optional and not just for a Sunday morning church service. If we do not possess these traits, we are blind to eternal things. They will save us from ineffective, unproductive living, keep us from sin, and result in a rich reward in Heaven (verse 11). We dare not "leave home without them" each day!

VICTORY IN KNOWING JESUS

1. We must put every effort into our character development.
2. If we are alive, we will grow when fed the right nutrients (God's Word).
3. Positive character traits will make our lives productive.

123

Faith Based Upon Fact

We did not follow cleverly invented stories when we told you about the power and coming of our Lord Jesus Christ, but we were eyewitnesses of his majesty.

(verse 16)

THE LAST WORDS of a man reveal much about what he considers most vital. They express his greatest concerns or his deepest hope, for a man dies as he has lived. Note the famous last words of several well-known men from history:

Charles Dickens, the author: "I commit my soul to the mercy of God, through our Lord and Savior Jesus Christ."

Voltaire, the famous infidel, who spent most of his life fighting Christianity: "I am abandoned by God and man: I shall go to hell!"

John Wesley, the evangelist: "Best of all, God is with us!"

Hobbs, the atheist: "I am taking a fearful leap in the dark!"

Sir David Brewster, inventor of the kaleidoscope: "I will see Jesus. I shall see Him as He is. I have had the light for so many years. Oh, how bright it is! I feel so safe and satisfied."

Peter would soon die and he knew it (verse 14). The Lord Jesus Himself had told him that his death would glorify God (John 21:18, 19). Tradition says Peter was crucified with his head down. The words he writes in his second letter, because of his impending death, are very significant. His emphasis is on the Word of God in days of apostasy.

It is not cleverly invented stories, tradition, or legend upon which our faith is based. Our faith in Jesus is based upon historical facts of His life, death, resurrection, and ascension as recorded by eyewitnesses! We have *more* reason to believe in the authenticity of the gospel record than any other facts of history. Men don't really have an intellectual problem accepting the Word of God. They have a *sin* problem. When they are willing to repent of their sins and forsake them, they see the truth of the Word of God.

Not only were the apostles eyewitnesses of Jesus words and deeds, but God the Father spoke audibly to confirm His identity (verse 17). The occasion was called the "Transfiguration" (Luke 9:28-35). This experience was a foretaste of Jesus' appearance in glory and it made an indelible impression upon Peter, James, and John. Their appetites were wet for eternity and they could never forget His glory!

Finally, Peter says that we have prophecy fulfilled, which confirms God's Word. Of the 330 Old Testament prophecies concerning the first coming of Christ, all were fulfilled by Him!

All Scripture is "God-breathed" (2 Timothy 3:16). He transmitted His will and word through the personalities of the men He inspired to write. Every word of Scripture is inspired and was written not of man's will but of God's (2 Peter 1:20, 21). The Bible is the foundation of our faith. If the enemy can destroy the foundation, the whole structure crumbles. That is why there is such a great attack upon the authority, the inerrancy, and the inspiration of God's Word today. Many churches have become nothing more than social clubs because they have denied God's Word. For example, the December, 1990 issue of *Reader's Digest* reported that only 11 percent of clergy delegates to the 1988 United Methodist General Conference said they believed the Bible is "the literal Word of God." Because of apostasy ("falling away") in mainline denominations of our day, many renewal groups have sprung up to renew our commitment to Biblical Truth. In 1991, of the 500 fastest growing American churches, 445 do not belong to a mainline denomination.

The battle for the Bible is on. But God's Word has already won! Men do not break down God's Word, but instead break themselves on His Word. Thank God, the facts win every time!

VICTORY IN KNOWING JESUS

1. A man's last words are very significant.
2. Peter used his last words to affirm God's Word.
3. Our faith is based upon facts recorded by eyewitnesses.
4. *All* Scripture is inspired of God.
5. It is through God's written Word that we know what Jesus is like.

THE ATHLETE OF THE 90s

IF WE ARE to motivate athletes to achieve to their potential, we must understand the nature of man. Only when we understand who we are and who we are dealing with, can we accomplish the task of motivation to the highest level.

Who is man? The Scripture says man is made in the image of God (Genesis 1;26, 27). We are distinctly separate from the animals. We have body, soul, and spirit. We are a special creation, designed to please the Heavenly Father. We are loved by a wonderfully all-knowing, all-powerful, and everywhere present God. We were designed to be busy caring for the place God put us (Genesis 1:15). We were created to enjoy God and to enjoy life.

But man has bought the lie that we could be equal with God (Genesis 3:5). When man disobeyed God and went his own independent way, close communication with the Creator was lost. The Bible says, "Therefore just as sin entered the world through one man, and death through sin, and in this way death came to all men, because all have sinned" (Romans 5:12). Our hearts are deceitful above all things and beyond cure (Jeremiah 17:9). We can't even understand the depths of our own human depravity, but we know something is dreadfully wrong inside. All mankind is born with a sinful nature (Romans 3:23). Man is rebellious, wanting his own way. He not only instinctively rebels against God, but against all other authority as well. Studying rising crime rates, the Minnesota Crime Commission recently came to this conclusion:

> Every baby starts life as a little savage. He is completely selfish and self-centered. He wants what he wants when he wants it — his bottle, his mother's attention, his playmate's toy, his uncle's watch. Deny him these once, and he seethes with rage and aggressiveness which would be murderous were he not so helpless. He is dirty, he has no morals, no knowledge, no skills.
>
> This means that all children — not just certain children, all children — are born delinquent. If permitted to continue in the self-centered worlds of his infancy,

127

given free rein to his impulsive actions to satisfy his wants, every child would grow up a criminal — a thief, a killer, or a rapist.

God gave us His law as a mirror, so we could look at it and see how far we have fallen from His perfect righteousness (Galatians 3). We are made righteous before God when we see our sin and trust the blood of the innocent Lamb of God, Jesus Christ, to pay the debt we owe to a Holy God. Then, He counts us as righteous before Him! He gives us a nature that wants to please Him by doing what is right!

On our athletic teams, we will have players whose hearts are in rebellion against God and players who really want to please God. Sometimes the old nature of the righteous players dominates them temporarily and they act in rebellious ways also. Because of these old sinful natures, we must have agreed upon, enforced discipline (rules). There must be a "code of conduct," a "rule of ethics" enforced by the head coach. It need not be a long list, for sometimes the more rules we list the more the rebellious sinful nature resists them. There were only 10 original commandments given by God.

We know that positive reinforcement works better than negative reinforcement. Players work harder when praised than when constantly punished. If players follow guidelines and are praised, their motivation is greater. But no team always pleases their coach and no coach can please the entire team all the time. Some players must be pushed in practice to give more effort than their old sin nature wants to give, for laziness is one trait of that old nature. Other players have a greater problem with unrestrained tempers, backbiting, or selfishness. The old sinful nature is never satisfied and coaches must recognize this fact. It is wonderful when players willingly act according to a Godly value system, but if they do not, they must be held accountable (disciplined) for their own good and for the progress of the team.

We have assumed the coach is committed to Jesus Christ and walking in a way that pleases Him. Coaches also have a sinful nature which can cause a real problem! Let us love the Lord Jesus and live to please Him!

SPORTS AND VALUES
IN THE 90s

AS A JUNIOR HIGH, high school, or college coach, you occupy a crucial position in America during the 1990s. Our value system has come under attack from every side. Liberal theologians, radical feminists, and groups advocating such perverse things as the acceptance of sodomy as an alternate lifestyle bombard us through the media. Young people spend hours in front of television and video games as the ethic of hard work is drained from their consciousness. Many coaches feel that the athletic world may be the last stronghold of discipline in our culture.

Yet, the value of our games *depend upon how they are coached.* These values depend upon our personal values! If the coach has no strong convictions about right and wrong, his or her players are adversely influenced and participation may do more harm than good! But as we strive to promote godly character traits, we deeply affect the lives of youth in a positive direction. May we never buy the lie that an educational curriculum (or a sport) must be "value neutral." *A valueless education becomes a worthless education.* The role of the coach is critical.

From study after study, we know that athletic participation enhances academic achievement and keeps kids in high school. The myth of the "dumb jock" is just that — a myth. A Women's Sports Foundation survey of 13,481 students from 1980-86 demonstrated that high school athletes had higher grades, lower dropout rates, and more frequent college attendance than non-athletes, male and female. A 1984 Texas study of 56,140 randomly selected students showed that non-athletes failed courses at twice the rate of athletes. A Minnesota study that same year showed that athletes had overall higher grade point averages (2.84 to 2.68) than all students taken together. A 1980-91 Iowa study showed the same results, and a 1982-83 Kansas study showed that 94 percent of dropouts that year were non-athletes!

It is clear that athletics enhances education. The question is: What are we teaching kids in that educational curriculum? Are we diligent to teach positive moral values? If not, we waste our time. American coaches occupy some of the most crucial positions in the world today. Ours is a most high calling. Let's make the most of it!

COACHING FOR CHRIST
IN THE 90s

IS IT POSSIBLE to coach for Christ in the day in which we live? Can we order our priorities in such a way to please our Heavenly Father in everything we say and do? The answers to these questions will determine our joy and satisfaction in this life *and* the degree of our rewards in the next!

Certainly if Christians could stand for Jesus, even grow stronger in the persecution of Peter's day, we can stand for Him and grow stronger in a secular America today! As people committed to the Lord Jesus Christ, we must represent Him to players, fans, and parents. He said we are the light of the world and the salt of the earth (Matthew 5:13, 14). But He also warned us not to hide the light (verse 13) or lose our saltiness (verse 16).

The next section of this study will encourage you to live boldly for our Savior. It may be difficult. God never promises ease in this wicked world. But living with our eyes upon Him and with His goals and values is gloriously possible in every circumstance. The challenge for us is to join the growing "fraternity of committed Christian coaches in America," dedicated to the victory of the Lord Jesus Christ in their lives and in the lives of others.

Let's just do it!

COACHING
WHEN THE BOTTOM FALLS OUT

THE PRESSURES OF COACHING are as real for the committed Christian as they are for the coach who has no faith in Jesus Christ. But the Christian coach has a Source of strength which the world misunderstands and refuses to accept. Though pressures vary, all levels of coaching have their problems. As sport psychologist Thomas Tutko points out, "There is no place that problem behavior is more likely to occur than in athletes." Consider these examples and the men who have stood for Christ "when the bottom has fallen out" on them.

BOLDNESS IN WALK AND TALK

BILL McCARTNEY, Colorado football coach, knelt on the turf at Folsom Field and committed his program to the Lord Jesus Christ. He received much criticism for his bold position. Players of lesser character brought bad publicity to the program by off the field antics. Bill stood firmly against the murder of unborn babies (abortion) and suffered for that stance. When his quarterback got his own daughter pregnant, Bill not only forgave him, but led him to Christ just before the player died of cancer! The McCartneys daily prove the reality of their love and the sincerity of their pro-life position by helping raise the young grandchild.

McCartney has had scathing columns written about him by writers from around the country who have never even spoken to him. The American Civil Liberties Union has pressured him to quit leading team prayers and to stop witnessing openly for Christ. Yet, he not only has survived, but he has maintained a bold Christian witness while building a national power at the University of Colorado.

One of Bill McCartney's favorite verses is Romans 8:29: "For those God foreknew He also predestined to be conformed to the likeness of His Son, that He might be the firstborn among many brothers." "That tells us that our purpose is to conform to the image of Jesus Christ, and that singularly helps me keep a focus," he says. "That's what I'm called to do, and I should be gradually growing and changing. He should be increasing and I should be decreasing."

BELIEVING GOD IN GOOD TIMES AND BAD

GRANT TEAFF, 1974 National Coach of the Year says, "No matter what our age our walk of life, Jesus Christ should be the center of our lives." It was during that season that Teaff led the Bears to their first championship in 50 years. He has run a clean and competitive program year after year. But Coach Teaff is also living proof that "all who live godly lives in Christ Jesus shall suffer."

Teaff has suffered emotionally through the tragic death of a precious daughter of one of his star players, a 1975 season of critical injuries, sleepless nights and criticism during an 0-5 start in 1978, the insecurity of a continual one-year contract, the permanent paralysis of a sophomore defensive back during a practice session, the false accusations of recruiting violations, and an attack of multiple sclerosis in his daughter Tammy. Through the ups and downs of life, Grant Teaff has remained faithful to God and an inspiration to coaches of every sport in all parts of America.

MORE THAN WINNING

TOM OSBORNE, Nebraska's football coach, is the winningest active coach in NCAA Division. But his great success during 18 years at the helm has brought criticism from fans who expect a conference championship every year! Tom's 1985 open heart surgery has been another trial he has faced successfully, with the Lord's help.

Until Tom attended a Fellowship of Christian Athletes conference in Estes Park, Colorado, in 1957, much of what he "believed about God was a sort of second hand religion." "I'd gone to church, gone to Sunday School, and was what folks would call a 'religious person'," he says. "I returned from that conference more excited about Christianity. I had made an active, personal commitment. For the first time I had a true sense of where I was headed spiritually.

"I've gotten away from measuring success in terms of wins and losses," says Coach Osborne. "It's a mistake those of us in coaching too often make when we define a good season as winning a certain number of games or a championship.

"Therefore, it's made sense to me to measure success more in terms of how closely a team has come to realizing its potential. As a result, I've almost never talked to a team about setting a goal of winning a particular football game, but of getting into *position* to win the game. The important thing is to play the best we are able to play. If we do that, we should be able to live with the consequences."

ON THE FIRING LINE

SPACE DOES NOT PERMIT a detailed summary of godly coaches who have been harassed and/or fired. It happened to Tom Landry, a legend in pro football, when a new owner bought the Dallas Cowboys and hired a personal friend with a different philosophy to replace him.

Another Christian coach was on a recruiting trip and was called to be told he was replaced. The reason was that the school found a bigger "name" with which to promote its program! Yet, the replaced coach was "Coach of the Year" the previous season!

Still another man was harassed by the ACLU and told he could not use "Christian principles in his decision-making process." Another coach had been an unpaid volunteer for 3 years at a Division I school, and was passed over when a full-time slot became available. Others have suffered winless seasons, but still served God with character and dignity.

The bottom can fall out on any career! But the Christian coach has a foundation more firm than any coaching job. His foundation is the person of the Lord Jesus Christ. And that foundation stands solid as a rock!

Seeking God's Coaching Job

Father,

I come to You in the name of Jesus, my Lord and Savior. He is my only Righteousness and my sure Redemption. It is His cause for which I live and His agenda which I will follow.

I acknowledge that He knows what is best for me. I have not the wisdom, strength, or ingenuity to obtain or maintain the job where I can best be used for His glory on the earth. Icompletely yield my life to Him for His purposes from now until I leave this earth. I forsake my own agenda, my selfish plans, my greedy motives. I allow you to surgically remove all the cancer of selfish desires, whatever the cost. You may refine my life however it pleases You.

Father, I believe you have left me physically on the earth for a reason. I seek Your glory in my work. Sovereignly lead me to a job of your choosing in Your timing. Since promotion comes not from any earthly direction but only from You (Psalm 75:6, 7), I ask you to act. Since you are the One who lifts up or sets down even the rulers of nations, You are the One who has the power and right to place me.

You have told us to work to provide for the needs of our families. I want to be your tool to evangelize the world in which I live. Give me great grace in doing these things. I am helpless to obtain on my own. By faith, I will apply for jobs which may be Your will. By faith I will keep on asking, seeking, and knocking. But only You can release that place where I ought to be at this time. Create great favor for me in the heart of an employer. Turn his heart to me and open the way to use the job as a platform to share the love of Jesus Christ with other coaches and teams. Save thousands through the revival You begin in my place of influence. You take all the glory. I make the commitment to never take for myself Your glory in doing these things.

In the Mighty Name of Jesus, Amen.

135

VIII. Faithful Living in Difficult Days

GOD HAS a purpose for everything He allows to come into our lives and a plan to go with it. One day we'll see it all fit together.

2 Peter 2

Days of False Teachers (verses 1—3) • **139**
The Judgment of False Teachers
    (verses 4—9) • **141**
Description of False Teachers (verses 10—16) • **142**
Sows vs. Sons (verses 17—22) • **144**

☆ ☆ ☆ ☆ ☆ ☆
Coaching Clinic: The Authority of God's Word
☆ ☆ ☆ ☆ ☆ ☆

The Authority of God's Word • **146**
Don't Be Faked Out by False Teachers • **148**
How to Choose a Church • **151**
Prayer: Strongholds • **153**

Days of False Teachers

But there were also false prophets among the people, just as there will be false teachers among you.

(verse 1)

GOOD COACHES spend much time teaching the fundamentals of their game. For example, in fielding a ground ball the hands must be out in front of the body, the knees bent, the body in front of the ball, and the rear end must stay down. Any departure from these principles spells trouble, usually failure. Coaches who teach fundamentals are considered "fundamentalists." Some coaches are very good teachers of the fundamentals and others are very poor.

One of the difficulties of our spiritual walk today is the false teachers that have sprung up everywhere. Peter warned of them. In the past, when God gave prophets to Israel, there were false prophets sent by Satan. Today, because God uses teaching to build the church, Satan has sent false teachers to confuse us. A false teacher is one who knows the truth and deliberately lies for some reason. His motive may be to gain a following or to please the people, but it is more often money. These false teachers are *in* the church, not *outside* it. They are successful numerically, for Peter says, "many" will follow their shameful ways (verse 2). They claim to be Christians, but deny the fundamentals. Because the errors they teach are so widespread, the truth is despised. For example, the term "fundamentalist" is slandered today, as false teachers try to make teachers of truth look foolish.

These false teachers introduce destructive heresies into the church. Included among these teachers are the "Word of Faith" teachers, who teach that if you have enough faith to claim it, God must grand your every whim. There are the "positive thinkers" who try to build man's self-esteem without the cross of Jesus. Some promote the false idea that we must turn off our minds and be ruled by what our "hearts" tell us. The "seed-faith" preachers promise us money from God if we send them money first. Some "faith-healers" teach that it is always God's will to heal us now. Others teach the idea of "revelation knowledge" given supernaturally outside God's Word. And there are those who actually claim to be God, pray to themselves, and tell us that we, too, are God. We easily recognize cults such as the Jehovah's Witnesses, Mormons, and Christian Scientists, but these subtle ideas infiltrate our churches and deceive many weak believers.

Peter writes that these false teachers "deny the Lord who bought them." Does this mean that they were saved and then lost? No. All men were bought by Christ's blood, but many are never saved because they do not apply that blood to themselves. His blood is *sufficient* for all men to be saved, but *efficient* only for those who personally accept Him. The false teachers Peter writes about were never saved, even though they might have taught some things that are true. Every false system has *some* truth in it or nobody would be tricked into following its leader! Satan isn't stupid, after all!

False teachers are ferocious wolves in sheep's clothing (Matthew 7:15, Acts 20:29). But Jesus said those who are really His sheep hear His voice and follow Him (John 10:27). As believers in Jesus, we need not be fooled by any false preacher or teacher, for we have God's Word and His Holy Spirit to teach us truth. We can stick to the fundamentals and be kept from error in every game!

FAITHFUL LIVING IN DIFFICULT DAYS

1. Many false teachers are teaching in churches today.
2. Money (greed) is the motive of most false teachers.
3. We are kept safe from false teachers by studying the fundamentals of God's Word (and sticking to them).

The Judgment of False Teachers

. . . the Lord knows how to rescue godly men from trials and to hold the unrighteous for the day of judgment, while continuing their punishment.

(verse 9)

JUDGMENT WAS CERTAIN for Pete Rose. For some time it was rumored that he was involved in illegal gambling. Evidence continued to mount, but arrest and conviction was delayed. Pete continued to manage and the pressure increased. Finally, in 1990, he was arrested, tried, and convicted of his illegal activities. He was sent to prison and served community service time to pay for his actions. Judgment day took some time for Pete, but it was certain.

Another Peter wrote of God's certain judgment of ungodly, false teachers and His sure rescue of the righteous. Peter used three examples to emphasize that the ungodly will not escape. First, God judged the one-third of the angels who rebelled against Him when they followed Lucifer. They were divested of all their glory and some of the worst were sent to hell to be held in chains of darkness until their final judgment in the Lake of Fire.

Second, God once destroyed everything with a worldwide flood, while saving only righteous Noah and his family. Noah's world was terribly violent. It was a world where men had gotten so low that every inclination of the thoughts of their hearts was only evil *all* the time (Genesis 6:5). God was left out of man's religion in that day. The Lord's judgment showed His care for the future of man, for had it not been for one righteous man, there would have been no salvation for any man of all time! From the flood, we learn that false teachers will not escape God's judgment because of their great numbers. He once wiped out the whole world because of sin! The majority can be (and often is) wrong!

Third, God destroyed Sodom and Gomorrah by fire because of their homosexuality. When men descend to that level, they have become lower than animals. God gives them over to their depravity and the consequences (Romans 1:18—32). That's why many are so hard and hateful. Physical death occurs because their natural immunity fails (AIDS) as surely as spiritual death has resulted from separation from God. It is a dangerous choice to reject God's love for man's lust.

God's judgment of false teachers is as sure as His judgment of demons, violent men, and homosexuals. But in judgment of the ungodly, He always remembers to rescue the righteous. Noah and Lot remind us of God's care for righteousness. If we choose His way, He will save us from whatever is ahead.

FAITHFUL LIVING IN DIFFICULT DAYS

1. God cares enough about man to judge evil.
2. God's judgment is sure.
3. God knows how to rescue the righteous.

---

2 Peter 2:10—16

Description of False Teachers

But these men blaspheme in matters they do not understand.
(verse 12)

PHYSICAL PAIN is the athlete's warning system to prevent damage to muscles, tendons, and ligaments. That's why it can be dangerous for a pitcher to either ignore an ache in the elbow or to deaden the pain with a drug. The pain is a symptom of overuse or damage of some sort. Just as one would not continue driving a car with the oil light flashing, neither should we ignore sharp pain in a joint.

God has given several "warning lights" flashing around false teachers of religion. These are given to warn His people of the danger of being influenced by evil men who pose as church officials, for the real dividing line between good and evil is not geographical or political, but is in the human heart! False teachers follow their own sinful natures (verse 10) instead of God's Spirit. They refuse to be held accountable by anyone and go off on their own, despising authority (verse 10). No slander of anyone is allowed in God's presence, but they slander beings they do not understand. Even angels do not accuse fallen angels to God (See Jude 9). Peter warned that false teachers live instinctively instead of rationally. They live like beasts and like beasts, will be destroyed (verse 12). Evidently, Peter felt heresy was serious, and he didn't downplay its consequences!

The false teachers of Peter's day didn't even try to hide their blatant sin. Like many today, they thought of sex every time they saw a woman. They were driven by greed, following the "way of Balaam," a mercenary prophet who, for a fee, urged the Moabites to ensnare God's people by tricking their men into illicit sexual relations (Numbers 22). Even today, money and sex in the name of religion brings spiritual ruin. Religion for profit is the motive of many preachers. An extravagant lifestyle is one mark of such greed-driven men and women.

Thank God, He gives us a "warning light" to alert us to false doctrine. And, thank God, we have His Word to check out the accuracy of the unscrupulous.

FAITHFUL LIVING IN DIFFICULT DAYS

1. The dividing line of good/evil is in the human heart.
2. False teachers are driven by greed and lust.
3. We have God's Word to warn us and keep us away from false teachers.

Sows vs. Sons

A sow that is washed goes back to her wallowing in the mud.

(verse 22)

THERE HAVE BEEN some famous predictions that have proven to be way off the mark. For example, the first time Jackie Gleason saw Elvis Presley perform, he said, "I tell you flatly — he won't last." Or, how about General Custer's remark just before meeting Sitting Bull at the Little Big Horn: "I guess we'll get through with them someday." Or, consider the prediction of D. W. Griffith, the famous film maker who said in 1924, "There will never be talking pictures." And after a new fabric was introduced to England in 1912, a British silk manufacturer stated, "It will never catch on. No one will ever accept artificial silk." The material was rayon.

False predictions in the spiritual realm are made by false teachers. Peter gives us a further description of false teachers. He says they are springs without water, mists driven by a storm. They appear to be real, but are only a mirage. They look like they'll deliver needed refreshment, but never deliver it. They withhold the Word of God from thirsty people who sit and listen to them. As a result, great numbers of spiritually thirsty people have deserted the cold, formal, liberal churches of today.

Second, false teachers use high sounding religious words but have no depth or substance in what they say. They have a religious education without a regenerated heart. They have a head knowledge of Jesus, but no love for Him. Many preachers have nice, socially acceptable churches and they have escaped the seamy side of life (corruption) in the world. But they turn their backs on Jesus, the Way of righteousness. Eventually, such men return to their true, natural condition because they were never changed into sons of God on the inside. They resemble cleaned-up pigs. In fact, J. Vernon

McGee calls this section the *Parable of the Prodigal Pig,* based upon the Parable of the Prodigal Son (Luke 15).

The story of the prodigal son recounts how a kind father's son demanded his portion of the rich father's inheritance, lost it in sinful living and ended up slopping pigs for a meager existence. One day, he realized his foolishness and returned to his father to seek forgiveness and reconciliation. Because he was a *son,* he could not stay in the pig pen! But no pig would stay out of the pig pen for good! We could take him out of the mud and muck, scrub him, anoint him with perfume, tie a nice bow around his neck and bring him into the father's house. But the pig is never happy in the house of the kind father. He is not a son, but still a pig! One day, when he sees the opportunity, the pig will bolt out the door and head back to his real home — the mud and ooze of the pig pen — and his real father (the devil). He jumps right back into sin and feels at home again, for his heart was never regenerated and his old nature never changed!

Such is the case with false teachers and their victims. They may "clean up their act" for a while, join a church, get baptized and do some good deeds, but until they put their trust in Jesus Christ and become sons of God, they are outside God's family. Eventually, they return to a lifestyle that reveals their true character. Better for them to have no knowledge of righteousness, than to have heard and rejected it!

FAITHFUL LIVING IN DIFFICULT DAYS

1. False teachers leave Jesus out of their religion.
2. A son is never happy in a pig pen.
3. A pig is never at home in the Father's presence.
4. Sons and pigs are eventually exposed by their conduct.

145

THE AUTHORITY OF GOD'S WORD

MODERN LIBERAL THEOLOGIANS have waged a relentless attack on the authenticity of God's Word. This attack is nothing new. It was begun by Satan in the Garden of Eden when he asked Eve, "Did God *really* say, 'You must not eat from any tree of the garden?'" He followed that attack with a direct contradiction of God's Word. "You will not surely die," said Satan (Genesis 3:1—5). How history has exposed Satan as a liar and man as a "piece of cake" for accepting his lies!

All writers of the gospels in the New Testament were *eyewitnesses* of the events about which they wrote. They came from varied backgrounds, yet all agree in detail! Today we have almost 5,000 ancient Greek manuscripts of the New Testament. Yet, 1500 years after Herodotus, known as the "Father of History," wrote his history there is only one copy in the entire world! Twelve hundred years after Plato wrote his classic, there remains only one manuscript. Very few manuscripts of Sophocles, Euripedes, Virgil, Cicero, Pliney, Julius Caesar, and Aristotle exist. There is more evidence for the authenticity of the New Testament than for almost any 10 pieces of classical literature combined! And the New Testament (especially Jesus Himself) quotes extensively from the Old Testament — a fact confirming its authenticity as well.

Scientifically speaking, the Bible confirms the earth is round (Isaiah 40:22), suspended in space (Job 26:7), the stars are innumerable (Genesis 15:5), there are mountains and canyons in the sea (2 Samuel 22:16), the hydrologic cycle (Ecclesiastes 1:6, 7), and the invisible atom (Romans 1:20) — all before man discovered these things. God established health and sanitation laws and outlined thermodynamic principles for man's use far before we "discovered" their existence.

Literally hundreds of Biblical prophecies have been fulfilled. Many more are being and will be fulfilled. What a help to us today as we plan for future events in a chaotic world! The universal influence of Scripture upon civilization, the arts, law, government, and education has been profoundly good. Where would the world be without God's Word?

The Bible does not cover up flaws in the character of God's men and women. Noah, Moses, David, Elijah, and Peter all had major weaknesses. If man had written the book in an effort to start a religion, he would have edited the evil in these lives. God tells it like it is about man's helpless condition apart from His grace.

Most significantly, the life-transforming power of the Book proves it to be God's Word. Men and women who formerly ridiculed God and Christians have laid down their lives for God and His Word. No evil or murderous dictator has ever been a friend of the Bible and no good and wise leader has ever been an enemy of the Bible! God's Word is true. It changes lives for good. And it has stood the test of time.

DON'T BE FAKED OUT
BY FALSE TEACHERS

. . . having a form of godliness but denying its power. Have nothing to do with them.

2 Timothy 3:5

PAUL WROTE to Timothy to warn him that in the last days false teachers would invade the church. Timothy was to have nothing to do with them. Today, we have the same problem. From whom would Paul advise *us* to turn away? It is relatively easy to identify the errors in the world's major religions. After all, the founders of Hinduism, Buddhism, and Mohammedanism are all dead! Their tombs are all occupied. Jesus Christ — the Way, the Truth and the Life (John 14:6) — is risen from the dead! He lives today, and that fact validates all His claims! But it would take volumes to list all the cults that have emerged from distortions of Biblical Christianity. And 80 percent of cultists used to be involved with orthodox Christian churches. This is not an attack upon them. They are the ones who left and now attack Biblical Christianity!

What is a cult? A cult is a group of persons gathered around a magnetic *personality* or his *interpretation* of Scripture. Every cult *denies Christ* as God in human form who died for the sins of mankind. False prophets of the cults do not look, act, or sound like false prophets. It is possible to live moral and ethical lives on the surface and be at war with a holy God. Jesus said we'd know them by their fruits. Fruit means not only the life that is lived, but also the doctrine that is taught!

Unitarianism is one of America's biggest cults in practice. It denies the incarnation of Jesus Christ and rejects His claims. This "religion of the intellect" has captured many professional people in our country. Their teaching is basically, "God helps those who help themselves."

Freemasonry (and all groups under its control) base their rites upon ancient pagan and Satanic rituals. Their humanistic teachings are in opposition to God's Word.

148

Anyone involved with Freemasonry in any form should compare its teaching with the Word of God.

Armstrong's "Worldwide Church of God" is a cult which claims to be teaching the only true gospel of Christ to the whole world. This group has sidetracked many Christians by misapplying and misinterpreting Biblical truth.

The cult of Mormonism is internally contradictory. Among its teaching are that we can become Gods (as they say God became a God), that there are many Gods in Heaven who have wives, and that there is no salvation outside their church. They are dedicated, loyal to those inside their group, and successfully growing numerically.

Likewise, the Jehovah's Witnesses, who deny or refuse to recognize the Trinity, the Diety of Jesus Christ, His bodily resurrection, His blood atonement, and His second coming are not difficult to recognize as a cult. These are all basic Biblical truths. Any other teacher, no matter how closely identified with Christianity, must be examined by the same criteria. It is appalling how many popular teachers (some on TV) believe that no one can interpret Scripture for himself, are man-centered, deny Biblical orthodoxy, are greedy for monetary gain, and present themselves as mediators between God and man! Christians must be careful who they listen to and to whom they send money!

Probably the fastest growing worldwide cult today is the New Age Movement. It is made up of hundreds of networking groups, not all of which are even aware of their leaders' agenda! This movement is designed to include anyone and everyone — except Biblical Christians — in one worldwide religion. Various names are used for the movement, including The Aquarian Conspiracy, New Consciousness, Cosmic Humanism, Cosmic Consciousness, Mystical Humanism, Human Potential Movement, and Holistic Health Movement, among others. Buzz words include centering, higher consciousness, enlightenment, global village, spaceship earth, transcendental, and others. Symbols include: the rainbow, pyramid, the triangle, an eye in a triangle, a swastika, the yin and yang, the unicorn, goat's heads, crystals, and pentagrams.

149

Though not everyone who uses these symbols is a New Ager or an occultist, frequent use of these symbols should alert Christians. Beliefs include the concept of an impersonal God, human potential and goodness, usefulness of sorcery (mind-manipulation), a "Christ-consciousness" (but not the historical Jesus), mystical feelings, and a unity of all religions and all governments.

Since both Paul and Peter have warned us of false teachers, we have no reason to be taken in by them. Let us grow closer to our Lord Jesus every day by becoming more knowledgeable of His Word. Only then can we discern the truth from Satan's falsehoods.

HOW TO CHOOSE A CHURCH

And all who believed were together.

Acts 2:44

CHRISTIANITY is a team sport. But the question is often asked, "How do I choose a good church?" The following may help in your evaluation.

1. The Word — Look for a church where the Bible is taken seriously, taught clearly and applied practically (2 Timothy 3:14—17).

2. The People — Look for people who are responsive to the claims Christ makes upon them in His Word. Our religion shouldn't be something we put on and take off with our Sunday clothes. Ask yourself if the people in this church live in continuous repentance and faith and are maturing in character. Most of all, do they love one another? (John 14:15)

3. The Ministry — Look for a church that will train you to serve. "If I attend this church, will I improve as a student, coach, servant, friend, example, family member?" A good church should treat you as a responsible person capable of ministering and it should hold you accountable for that ministry. (1 Timothy 4:7, 8).

4. The Mission — Look for a church that's not only a taker but a giver. Some fellowships become ingrown; people come to a service to get a blessing but give no thought to leaving to be one. Ask yourself, "Do they sacrifice their time, money and talents to see that others at home and abroad experience the gospel?" (Matthew 28:18—20).

5. The Cults — Beware of the ever present cults. These false churches take from or add to the Bible. Their focus is upon an earthly leader who sets himself up as a dictator. Converts are turned away from family and friends. The cults teach that salvation isn't by faith alone, grace alone or Christ alone, and often they deny the Trinity and the deity of Christ. Members are more robots than loving, free people who trust God (Matthew 7:15—29).

6. The Nonessentials — Don't be turned off by a church because all your expectations aren't met. Things like buildings, order of worship, age of pastor, denominational tags and style of music are nonessentials (1 Timothy 4:12). Your motto should be, "In Essentials — Unity, In Nonessentials — Freedom, In All Things — Love."

7. The Demonstration — Find a church that's a "house of prayer" for all people (Mark 11:17). The early church brought together in one community the young and old, rich and poor, black and white, new convert and aged saint. And what a witness it was to the world! Such churches today also demonstrate the kingdom of God among us.

Finally, there's no such thing as a perfect church. If you do find one, stay away or you'll mess it up! Consider it enough to find an encouraging group of Christians who huddle together regularly and try to faithfully move in the direction Christ leads. With you in there working together with them, you can put "points on the board" for the cause of Christ.

Strongholds

Father,

Today I realize that the enemy has many strongholds with which to keep men prisoner to do his will. I am becoming more informed and therefore not ignorant of his devices. I come into Your presence fully aware of my dependence upon You and of Your complete adequacy to break down all barriers to the love of Jesus being shed abroad into men's hearts by the Holy Spirit.

In my own life, I cast down every imagination and every high thing that exhalts itself against the knowledge of God. May nothing in my life come between You and me. I confess all my pride, which has caused me to think more highly of myself than I ought to think. I confess greed in wanting the biggest and best for myself. I confess selfish ambition to make self look good in the eyes of others. Please forgive me, Father, and may Jesus be truly Lord of every part of my life.

O Lord, please break the Satanic strongholds of educational deception in my life and in our school system. Break the pride that comes from earned degrees that make us feel superior to others. Please destroy the teaching of the lie of evolution, which causes students to feel unaccountable to You, our Creator. How foolish we have been to take glory from You by crediting life to blind chance in a primevel soup!

Please break the Satanic stronghold of the role confusion of men and women in America. Our culture is so confused. (For wives) I confess that I have not submitted to the authority of my husband in everything You have commanded in Your Word. (For husbands) I confess that I have not loved my wife as Christ loved the church. Please forgive us and help us to turn from our wicked ways. As coaches, help us to become role models of your plan for marriage in our school. May our athletic program contribute to the development of manly young men and godly young ladies.

Finally, we tear down the stronghold of sexual perversion in our school. We confess our lust for those other than our spouses. Father, please break the addiction of sex outside of marriage in our school. Heal those who hurt so badly because of their own sin. Break the stronghold of pornography which holds captive the minds of many. Bind the demonic spirit of homosexuality which entraps others. Make clear to the heart of every man, woman and child the cure for AIDS — a man marrying and being faithful to one woman for life and vice versa. We have sinned. We are guilty of breaking ourselves when we break your laws.

Father, I thank You that no weapon formed against you shall prosper as You break these strongholds. Thank you for setting us free.

In the Name of Jesus, Amen.

IX. Return of the Lord

COACHES AND ATHLETES have great influence. We must be careful how we use it. Jesus said it would be better to have a large millstone hung around our necks and be drowned in the depths of the sea than to cause a little one to sin.

Matthew 18:2—6

2 Peter 3

Scoffers in the Last Days (verses 1—9) • **157**
The Day of the Lord: We Win! (verses 10—13) • **159**
On Guard and Growing (verses 14—18) • **160**

☆ ☆ ☆ ☆ ☆ ☆
Coaching Clinic: Assurance & Sharing Christ
☆ ☆ ☆ ☆ ☆ ☆

Assurance of Your Salvation • **162**
How to Prepare Your Personal Testimony • **170**
How to Pray • **171**
How to Lead Someone to Christ • **173**
Prayer: Open Doors to Share Christ • **175**

Scoffers in the Last Days

First of all, you must understand that in the last days scoffers will come, scoffing and following their own evil desires.

(verse 3)

FEW PEOPLE remember the 1927 Vanderbilt-Texas football game in Austin, Texas. On one pass play, officials were trying to decide whether a pass from Commodore quarterback Bill Spears had hit a player ineligible to receive it. The player was All-Southern center Vernon Sharp. Finally, they asked Sharp. He said "yes," it had hit him. The call went against Vandy, and Texas won 13—7. It was Vanderbilt's only 1927 defeat.

Sharp's honesty would be scoffed and ridiculed in today's "win at any cost" society. Many would reject him as clearly as they reject and ridicule Jesus' promise to return to put down evil and reign in glory. Peter wrote about these scoffers who follow their own evil desires. They are not only atheists, but some are church members. Some of them are pastors who deny the authority and accuracy of God's Word.

Jesus promise, "In my Father's house are many rooms; if it were not so, I would have told you. I am going there to prepare a place for you, I will come back and take you to be with me that you also may be where I am" (John 14:2, 3).

What is God's agenda? He is going to destroy the world. He destroyed the *past* world with a global flood because of mans continual sin (Genesis 6). There is abundant evidence of such a flood and that all things have not continued as they are since the day of creation. The *present* world God has reserved for a day of judgment (verse 7). We know the destruction of this world will be by fire (verse 7), but we don't know exactly how or when it will be touched off. Man will not and can not destroy the earth on his own, for God has reserved it for *His* judgment in *His* time. He will then bring a new world into being, the *future* world where Jesus reigns in righteousness (verse 13).

The days between Jesus' first and second coming are called the "last days." It seems like it's been a long time since Jesus promised to return to earth and the "last days" began. It's been almost 2000 years, but as God reckons time, it's only a day or two (Psalm 90:4). Aren't you glad He waited for you to be born and to be saved so you can go to Heaven to be with Him? He is in no hurry, for He existed in eternity past and will be here in eternity future!

God is concerned about those who scoff at His promise to return. Though they deliberately forget about His creation and past judgment by the flood, He loves them as much as He loves every person. And He is concerned about you. He is not wanting anyone to perish (verse 9). His will is that everyone repent of their sins and be saved. You can't keep God from loving you, but like using an umbrella in a rain storm, you can shield yourself with sin so you will never experience God's love. Why not believe Him instead of those who scoff at Him?

RETURN OF THE LORD

1. Peter wrote to stimulate us to wholesome thinking (verse 1).
2. Scoffers of God's promise were predicted long ago.
3. Those who ridicule God's promises deliberately forget His power in creation and judgment.
4. God must judge the earth by fire one day, for He has promised to do it!
5. God withholds immediate judgment to give men time to repent of their sin and be saved.

The Day of the Lord: We Win!

But the day of the Lord will come like a thief. The heavens will disappear with a roar; the elements will be destroyed by fire, and the earth and everything in it will be laid bare.

(verse 10)

TENNIS LINESWOMAN Dorothy Cavis-Brown proved to be a very ineffective judge during a Wimbledon match on June 22, 1964. While American Clark Graebner and South African Abe Segal were volleying, she dozed in her chair and leaned to one side. Graebner nudged her to see whether she had died. She awoke and probably felt like dying — of embarrassment!

Our God is not like a sleepy tennis lineswoman. He has already selected a day when He will destroy the earth by fire. It will be a sudden, catastrophic event and it will occur in God's time. We don't know when He has decreed to do it, but we know He always keeps His appointments! What He says, He will do! He never sleeps on the job. In the past, God destroyed the earth by water. The Bible says that "the springs of the great deep burst forth and the floodgates of the heavens were opened (Genesis 7:11). Rain fell for 40 consecutive days and everything not in the ark God provided was destroyed. But when the day of the Lord comes, He will use fire to destroy the earth. The oxygen and hydrogen (water) that comprises three-fourths of the earth will explode. We know of certain fires today that are only magnified by water, so scientifically, we know it is possible. The very elements will melt in the heat!

What a powerful incentive to live for God now! We know that this world will be destroyed and that God is preparing a new heaven and a new earth (verse 13)! Only righteousness dwells there. What a great new world that will be! There will be no more death, mourning, crying or pain (Revelation 21:1—4).

Righteousness is not at home on the earth today. Things are very unfair. Shakespeare described our world when he wrote in *Hamlet*, "The times are out of joint." In our language, they are "messed up." These are evil days. But one day, God will straighten everything out. When "His day" arrives, no one will mistake it!

RETURN OF THE LORD

1. God will destroy this world some day.
2. In God's new world, only righteousness will dwell.
3. "God's day" will come "as a thief."
4. Looking forward to "God's day" should motivate us to holy living.

---

2 Peter 3:14—18

On Guard and Growing

But grow in the grace and knowledge of our Lord and Savior Jesus Christ. To him be glory both now and forever! Amen.

(verse 18)

DID YOU KNOW that a future heavyweight boxing champion was once disqualified for not throwing a single punch in a bout? Sweden's Ingemar Johansson was fighting in the gold medal bout of the 1952 Olympic Games in Helsinki. Instead of fighting as he should, Johansson spent all his time back-pedaling from H. Edward Sanders of the United States. He was disqualified in Round 2 for "not giving of his best."

There are certain things that we must do if we are to live lives pleasing to God. We don't dare "not give of our best" in living for Him and growing in Him! Peter assumes that we are looking forward to the new heavens and new earth which God has promised (verse 14). Because our priorities are not in things of this world, he tells us to make every effort to live lives that are pure before our Heavenly Father. Too many folks put *no* effort into living for God. In contrast, we are to "bust our tails" to please God!

Not only are we to make every effort to please Him, but we must be "on guard" (verse 17) against the false teaching of so many who call themselves Christians. We are bombarded with cults in the name of religion. Many religious leaders use the same terms as believers in Jesus use, but they do not mean the same thing as we mean! We are to test everything that is taught by what the Word of God says. Yes, some truths are hard to understand. Either they are not fully revealed to us yet, or they are so great and wonderful that our limited, finite minds cannot grasp them. Often, ungodly teachers twist and distort these truths to gather a following for their own sake. We must stay on guard against such deception.

Peter closes with the key verse of this entire letter (verse 18). He says we are to "grow in the grace and knowledge of our Lord and Savior Jesus Christ." We will not stay static. We will grow or we will become "stunted" in our walk with Jesus. We gain knowledge by studying God's Word. Though many do not understand God's Word when they read it, the Bible can be understood with the help of the Holy Spirit. We must approach it with humility, knowing God has something to say to us. We will grow in grace as we apply His Word to every situation of life. To Him be glory — now and forever! Amen!

RETURN OF THE LORD

1. We are to work at our walk with Jesus.
2. Some of God's truth is hard to understand.
3. Ignorant and unstable people purposely distort God's Word.
4. We are to guard what we know to be truth and grow in grace and knowledge of Jesus.

ASSURANCE OF YOUR SALVATION

WITH SO MUCH uncertainty in our culture and with feelings bobbing up and down like a yo-yo, people sometimes have doubts in their minds about their salvation. These come from a variety of sources, mostly from Satan and self. Dr. Lee Bendell has prepared the following summary to answer those nagging fears that keep us from experiencing full peace and freedom in Christ.

Doubt #1:   I'm not *sure* I have salvation.

Answer: I either have or don't have salvation — there is no halfway status.

In reply Jesus declared, "I tell you the truth, unless a man is born again, he cannot see the kingdom of God."

John 3:3

For God so loved the world that he gave his one and only Son, that whoever believes in him shall not perish but have eternal life. For God did not send his Son into the world to condemn the world, but to save the world through him. Whoever believes in him is not condemned, but whoever does not believe stands condemned already because he has not believed in the name of God's one and only Son.

John 3:16—18

I tell you the truth, whoever hears my word and believes him who sent me has eternal life and will not be condemned; he has crossed over from death to life.

John 5:24

* I either believe or do not believe; I am either judged (condemned) or I am not judged (condemned).

Yet to all who received him, to those who believed in his name, he gave the right to become children of God.

John 1:12

• I have either received Christ or have not received Him.

He who has the Son has life; he who does not have the Son of God does not have life.

1 John 5:12

* I either have Christ or do not have Christ; I either have eternal life or I do not have eternal life.

***

Doubt #2: Sometimes the way I act makes me doubt my salvation.

Answer: My salvation is dependent only on faith — my believing — not on anything I do.

Therefore, since we have been justified through faith, we have peace with God through our Lord Jesus Christ.

Romans 5:1

For it is by grace you have been saved, through faith — and this not from yourselves, it is the gift of God, not by works, so that no one can boast.

Ephesians 2:8, 9

* My salvation is not dependent upon my "good works."

***

Doubt #3: I try to believe but I'm not really sure what to believe in — to have faith in — to really gain salvation.

Answer: The Bible answers that question.

ADMIT

For all have sinned and fall short of the glory of God.

Romans 3:23

For the wages of sin is death, but the gift of God is eternal life in Christ Jesus our Lord.

Romans 6:23

• I recognize myself as a sinner who deserves only death; but through faith in Christ, God offers me eternal life.

163

BELIEVE

For God so loved the world that he gave his one and only Son, that whoever believes in him shall not perish but have eternal life.

John 3:16

For what I received I passed on to you as of first importance: that Christ died for our sins according to the Scriptures.

1 Corinthians 15:3

Who is it that overcomes the world? Only he who believes that Jesus is the Son of God.

1 John 5:5

That if you confess with your mouth, "Jesus is Lord," and believe in your heart that God raised him from the dead, you will be saved.

Romans 10:9

If anyone acknowledges that Jesus is the Son of God, God lives in him and he in God.

1 John 4:15

* I believe God loves me so much that He sent His Son, Jesus Christ, to die for my sins, then raised Him from the dead.

REPENT

If we confess our sins, he is faithful and just and will forgive us our sins and purify us from all unrighteousness.

1 John 1:9

. . . But unless you repent, you too will perish.

Luke 13:3

* I am aware of and truly am sorry for my sins. I thank God for accepting Christ's death as the atonement for my sins and forgiving my sins.

RECEIVE

For, "Everyone who calls on the name of the Lord will be
saved."

Romans 10:13

Jesus answered, "I am the way and the truth and the life. No
one comes to the Father except through me.

John 14:6

* I now call on Jesus Christ to come into my heart and my
life. Thank you, God, for saving me and giving me eternal
life.

** You may wish to repeat the sentences above (*) as a
personal prayer to God — then write down the date and place
that you prayed this as a reminder of when you "got right
with God."

Doubt #4:   I do believe but I'm still not sure of my
salvation.

Answer: God will give me that assurance as I meditate in
His Word — for He wants me to know (without
question) His promise that I have salvation and
eternal life through faith.

And this is what he promised us — even eternal life.

1 John 2:25

I write these things to you who believe in the name of the Son
of God so that you may know that you have eternal life.

1 John 5:13

For you granted him authority over all people that he might
give eternal life to all those you have given him. Now this is
eternal life: that they may know you, the only true God, and
Jesus Christ, whom you have sent.

John 17:2, 3

165

That is why I am suffering as I am. Yet I am not ashamed, because I <u>know</u> whom I have believed, and am convinced that he is able to guard what I have entrusted to him for that day.

2 Timothy 1:12

Doubt #5: I don't seem to have "<u>proof</u>" of salvation in my life.

Answer: While there are some proofs of our salvation, the absence of these <u>proofs</u> is more evidence that we are not mature Christians rather than evidence that we don't have salvation.

PROOFS:

Therefore, if anyone is in Christ, <u>he is a new creation</u>; the old has gone, the new has come!

2 Corinthians 5:17

* I should see a <u>change</u> in my life.

We <u>know</u> that we have passed from death to life, <u>because we love our brothers</u>. Anyone who does not love remains in death.

1 John 3:14

No one has ever seen God; but <u>if we love each other</u>, God lives in us and his love is made complete in us.

1 John 4:12

* I should have a <u>loving attitude</u> toward my fellow Christians.

We <u>know</u> that we live in him and he in us, because <u>he has given us of his Spirit</u>.

1 John 4:13

The Spirit himself testifies with our spirit that we are God's children.

Romans 8:16

* The changes in my life are being brought about by God's Spirit.

For the message of the cross is foolishness to those who are perishing, but to us who are being saved it is the power of God.

1 Corinthians 1:18

We know that we have come to know him if we obey his commands.

1 John 2:3

* I have a new interest in reading and obeying God's Word.

THE REASON THESE PROOFS MAY BE ABSENT:

Brothers, I could not address you as spiritual but as worldly — mere infants in Christ.

1 Corinthians 3:1

* "Brothers" are Christians. They are in Christ, but are still "infants."

But I see another law at work in the members of my body, waging war against the law of my mind and making me a prisoner of the law of sin at work within my members.

Romans 7:23

. . . So then, I myself in my mind am a slave to God's law, but in the sinful nature a slave to the law of sin.

Romans 7:25

Therefore, there is now no condemnation for those who are in Christ Jesus, because through Christ Jesus the law of the Spirit of life set me free from the law of sin and death.

Romans 8:1, 2

* Even though as a Christian, I find myself sinning, I still have my salvation through faith and should have a constant attitude of wanting — in my mind — to serve God and attempting to rid myself of sin.

Doubt # 6: I'm sure I had salvation, but I think I <u>may have lost it</u>.

Answer: There are quite a number of things that would have to happen before I could "lose" my salvation.

. . . because I know whom I have believed, and am convinced that he is able to <u>guard</u> what I have entrusted to him for that day.

2 Timothy 1:12

* God's Word says He will <u>guard</u> and <u>keep</u> me. <u>God doesn't lie</u>.

Yes, and I ask you , loyal yokefellow, help these women who have contended at my side in the cause of the gospel, along with Clement and the rest of my fellow workers, <u>whose names are in the book of life</u>.

Philippians 4:3

* Somehow to lose my salvation, my <u>name</u> would have to be <u>taken out of the book of life</u>.

And you also were included in Christ when you heard the word of truth, the gospel of your salvation. Having believed, <u>you were marked in him with a seal, the promised Holy Spirit</u>.

Ephesians 1:13

* Somehow to lose my salvation, the <u>seal</u> of the Holy Spirit would have to be <u>broken</u>.

168

My sheep listen to my voice; I know them, and they follow me. I give them eternal life, and they shall never perish; <u>no one can snatch them out of my hand</u>. My Father, who has given them to me, is greater than all; no one can snatch them out of my Father's hand.

John 10:27—29

* Somehow to lose my salvation, I would have to be <u>snatched out of God's hand</u>.

For I am convinced that neither death nor life, neither angels nor demons, neither the present nor the future, nor any powers, neither height nor depth, nor anything else in all creation, <u>will be able to separate us from the love of God</u> that is in Christ Jesus our Lord.

Romans 8:38, 39

* There is no <u>power</u> that can come between me and God.

HOW TO PREPARE
YOUR PERSONAL TESTIMONY

EVERY COACH who knows Jesus Christ personally can have tremendous influence for Him if he will briefly share with others how he came to know the Lord. Coaches often have a chance to do this when speaking to various groups. In the space of 3 to 5 minutes, a coach can outline:

A. What my life was like before I received Christ. How I lived and thought. Be careful not to glorify the bad aspects as you reveal a part of the past.

B. How I received Christ. What were the circumstances surrounding your trusting Jesus? Make it simple.

C. Changes that took place after I received Christ. Close with a relevant verse.

Write out your testimony on a sheet of paper. Be honest and brief, but bold. Pray about what to say and then let it be known that He has saved you whenever you get the opportunity.

HOW TO PRAY

BELOW IS A PLAN OF PRAYER based upon the letters "A-C-T-S." It has been used effectively by groups and individuals to intercede with the Father.

Adoration:

The basic purpose of life is to give glory, honor and praise to God. Praise of Jesus Christ is the chief occupation of Heaven. Don't barge into the presence of Royalty! This part of prayer is all for God with nothing directed toward man. Worship Him, tell God you love Him, reflect upon His Goodness, His Greatness, His Names, His Power, His Majesty, and His Sovereignty.

1 Chronicles 29:11 • Revelation 4:11 • Psalm 34:1, 3
Nehemiah 9:6 • Isaiah 25:1 • Psalm 28: 6, 7
Psalm 146:18

Confession:

Make sure every sin is confessed, cleansed, and forgiven. To Confess means to "agree with." You called what you spoke an exaggeration — God calls it a Lie! You call it slang — God calls it Swearing. You call it simply repeating the truth you heard — God calls it Gossip. You call it a harmless social drink — God calls it Mistreating His Temple. You call it an addiction — God calls it Sin. Confession restores sweet fellowship with God.

Psalm 66:18 • 1 John 1:5—10

Thanksgiving:

Express your gratitude to God. Think of specific things to thank Him for: Your family, job, church, health, friends, daily provisions, His Word, freedom of worship, ability to approach Him through prayer and the like. Even thank Him for trials (1 Thessalonians 5:18). "Always give thanks . . ." (Ephesians 5:20).

1 Thessalonians 1:3 • Ephesians 1:16
Psalm 92:1 • Psalm 95:2

171

Supplication:

Make your petitions known to God. Supplication means "to ask for earnestly and humbly." Intercede boldly for others' needs, for your own needs, and for special needs.

Hebrews 4:16 • Daniel 9:3
Philippians 4:6 • Romans 1:10

Close your prayer time "in Jesus' name" (John 14:13). To pray in Jesus' name means to pray on the basis of all Jesus is and has done for us. We pray because He invited us to pray. We have confidence in Him because of His invitation. AMEN means "So be it, Lord." We rest our petitions in His powerful hands.

HOW TO LEAD
SOMEONE TO CHRIST

IF WE TRULY believe God's Word and we love our players, we'll have a desire to explain to them how they can know Jesus Christ in a personal way. Statistics say that 80 percent of those who trust Christ and stay in church are led to Him by a friend. Coaches qualify as a "friend" in this sense. Sadly, few church members are sharing Christ regularly! We can reverse this trend! Here are some helpful hints:

1. Remember success is not measured by the number you lead to Christ. God does the work as we obey Him by sharing His Word. Success is sharing Christ in His power and leaving the results to Him. This removes all pressure to "perform."

2. Many people really do not *know* how to become a Christian. If you take a few moments to explain the simplicity of the gospel, they will be *eternally* grateful.

3. Be prepared to make the gospel clear to those people God places in your path each day. Have a brief outline or plan in mind.

Appendix I, *The Winning Run*, is a brief, 4-point outline of the gospel in an athletic format. This is not the only way to present God's love (1st base), man's sin (2nd base), Jesus' death and resurrection (3rd base), and our need to receive Christ (home plate). But, it is a way. You can very simply lead a player to the Savior by reading through it with him. Remember, you are not just sharing an outline — you are explaining God's plan of salvation!

Here are some tips:

1. If questions arise that may change the subject, explain that it may be answered as you go through *The Winning Run*. Satan would try to divert one's attention from the real issue (salvation) as you share about Jesus Christ.

2. If the player seems unresponsive, do not be alarmed. Ask, "Does this make sense to you?"

3. Hold the book so the player can see it, or use two copies. You may even want to draw a diagram on a chalkboard.

4. When you come to the prayer, do not hesitate to ask whether it expresses his heart's desire. If so, ask whether he would like to pray the prayer out loud. Or ask, "Would you like to repeat the prayer after me as I read it?" Emphasize that the desire of one's heart is what matters and the words are only to verbalize that desire.

5. If the player does not want to pray to receive Christ, let him know you still love him. Thank him for giving you the opportunity to share such a great message of God's love and forgiveness. Let him take a copy of *The Winning Run* so he can refer back to it on his own time. You may say, "Before you go to sleep tonight, think about what we've discussed and listen to what God may say in His still, small voice."

6. If a player does pray to receive Christ, assure him that Christ came into his life as promised. Read 1 John 5:11—13 to assure him of his position in Christ:

And this is the testimony: God has given us eternal life, and this life is in his Son. He who has the Son has life; he who does not have the Son of God does not have life. I write these things to you who believe in the name of the Son of God so that you may know that you have eternal life.

1 John 5:11—13

What a great promise! God has given us eternal life and taken us into His family! Encourage your player to tell someone about his receiving Christ and to spend time each morning in God's Word. Help him secure a devotional guide to focus his attention and provide direction.

May God bless you as you share the good news of Jesus Christ!

Open Doors to Share Christ

Dear Father,

I thank You that You have sent us the Lord Jesus Christ, the only True Light in this dark world. Praise Your Name that You did not leave us in our blindness and sin, but sent Jesus to save us when we were so desperately lost! Thank You for the wonderful freedom to become a bondservant of the Master!

Lord, You have told us to go into all the world to preach your good news of salvation. This includes the athletic world. Blind and lost apart from Christ Jesus, the young people and parents of America need You so badly. You say that all who believe in You are not condemned, but those who believe not are already under sentence of condemnation to hell, eternally separated from You, because they have not believed in Your Son. Many love darkness rather than light because their deeds are evil.

Father, in line with Your plan, I pray that you would open doors that I may tactfully, yet boldly speak Your way of salvation by the blood of Jesus. I pray that You will free men from the bondage of death. May every place that the soles of my feet tread upon be given to me for the sake of Christ Jesus. I take this territory for You and Your kingdom. Men are in bondage to a "strong man" — Satan. You said that only after a strong man is bound can one "spoil his goods." I bind the "strong man" in Jesus' name and claim his slaves for Christ! Free the air waves from his dominance.

I also bind the religious demons who deceive men into thinking they are acceptable to God because of any ritual, good deeds, charitable donations, ceremony, family background, intellectual knowledge of Christianity, or emotional experience. May the evil deeds of these deceivers be exposed as men see themselves as You see them — hopelessly lost apart from Christ. May the truth of the gospel penetrate hardened hearts and melt them in Jesus' love. Convict men of sin, of the availability of Jesus' righteousness and of the reality of judgment to come by Your Holy Spirit.

In Jesus Name, Amen.

175

Appendices

BRETT BUTLER is an outspoken Christian who has starred for the Braves, Indians, Giants, and now the Dodgers. He is a real competitor who doesn't hesitate to share God's love and forgiveness when given the opportunity.

Appendix I

The Winning Run

PERHAPS YOU HAVE READ this book, but never personally trusted the Savior with your earthly life and your eternal destiny. The following baseball illustration explains how you can come to know the Lord Jesus Christ:

In baseball, a runner must touch all four bases to score a run for his team. The path to abundant and eternal life is very similar to the base paths on a ball diamond.

Step 1 (first base) along that path is realizing that God cares about you. He not only created you, but He also loves you very deeply. He is seeking to give you an abundant life now and for eternity.

For God so loved the world that He gave His one and only Son, that whoever believes in Him shall not perish but have eternal life.　　　　　　　　　　　　　　　John 3:16

I have come that they may have life, and have it to the fullest.

John 10:10

At second base **(step 2)** we admit that we are sinners and separated from God. He is perfect, pure, and good; we are not. Because by nature we disobey Him and resist Him, He cannot have fellowship with us without denying His goodness and holiness. Instead, He must judge us.

Whoever believes in Him is not condemned; but whoever does not believe stands condemned already, because he has not believed in the name of God's one and only Son.

John 3:18

We realize we can never reach God through our own efforts. They do not solve the problem of our sin.

For all have sinned and come short of the glory of God.

Romans 3:23

But your iniquities have separated you from your God; your sins have hidden His face from you, so that He will not hear.

Isaiah 59:2

For the wages of sin is death, but the gift of God is eternal life in Christ Jesus our Lord.   Romans 6:23

Third base is so close to scoring. Here **(step 3)** we understand that God has sent His Son, Jesus Christ, to die on the cross in payment for our sins. By His sacrifice, we may advance Home.

But God demonstrates His own love for us in this: While we were still sinners, Christ died for us.

Romans 5:8

For Christ died for sins once for all, the righteous for the unrighteous, to bring you to God.

I Peter 3:18

Jesus answered, "I am the way and the truth and the life. No one comes to the Father except through Me."

John 14:6

However, being CLOSE to Home does NOT count!

The Winning Run!

To score (step 4), we must personally receive Jesus Christ as Savior and Lord of our lives. We must not only realize that He died to rescue people from their sin but we must also trust Him to rescue us from our own sin. We cannot "squeeze" ourselves home any other way, and He will not force Himself upon us.

Yet to all who received Him, to those who believed in His name, He gave the right to become children of God.

John 1:12

For it is by grace you have been saved, through faith — and this is not from yourselves, it is the gift of God — not by works, so that no one can boast.

Ephesians 2:8-9

Why not receive Jesus Christ as your Savior and Lord right now? Simply say: "Yes, Lord," to His offer to forgive you for your sins and to change you.

_____
(signed)

_____
(date)

Tell someone of your decision and keep studying God's Word. These things greatly strengthen you (Romans 10:9-10). You may write *The Winning Run Foundation* for further encouragement. We would be thrilled to hear of your commitment! Welcome to eternal life!

Appendix II

The Perfect Reliever

THE FOLLOWING BASEBALL illustration explains how to walk consistently in the power of the Holy Spirit, our only hope for victory in spiritual warfare.

Have you confessed your sins and believed on the Lord Jesus Christ as your personal Savior? You must do this to be saved from eternal loss. Having done so, you have "scored the winning run," in the game of life.

So whoever has God's Son has life; whoever does not have His Son does not have life.
                    I John 5:12

YOU SIGNED WITH THE WINNING TEAM WHEN YOU RECEIVED CHRIST!

1. Your sins were forgiven (Colossians 1:14)
2. You became a child of God (John 1:12)
3. God indwelt you with His Spirit so you may live victoriously over the world (John 15:18-19), the flesh (Romans 7:15-18), and the devil (I Peter 5:8).
4. You began the process of discovering God's purpose for your life (Romans 8:29).

BUT....WHAT'S HAPPENING NOW?

Though our Lord has assured all His
children of eternal life (John 10:28) and our
position in Christ never changes, our practice
may sometimes bring dishonor to God. The
enemy rally makes life miserable.

The enemy's dugout:
Prayerlessness
No desire for Bible Study
Loss of love
Legalistic attitude
Jealousy
Guilt

This rally must be stopped, for the Bible makes it clear that
no one who belongs to God can continually practice sin
(I John 2:3; 3:6-10).

These two pitchers' mounds represent the two lifestyles from which a Christian must choose:

Self in control of the game
and Christ's Resurrection
power waiting in the bull-
pen — enemy rally pro-
duces discord.

For we naturally love to do
evil things that are just the
opposite from the things
that the Holy Spirit tells us
to do.

Power of Christ replaces
self on the mound — rally
is stopped and peace is
restored

... and the good things we
want to do when the
Spirit has His way with
us are just the opposite of
our natural desires.
Galatians 5:17a

SO WHAT'S THE SOLUTION?

184

BRING IN THE PERFECT RELIEVER!

We must step off the mound and allow God to have complete authority by giving control of the game to the Holy Spirit.

Only by giving the Holy Spirit of God His rightful place of authority over our every thought, word and deed, can we consistently overcome defeat and despair.

If we are living now by the Holy Spirit's power, let us follow the Holy Spirit's leading in every part of our lives.

Galatians 5:25

WHAT DOES THE HOLY SPIRIT DO?

When you received Jesus Christ as Savior, the Holy Spirit indwelt you (Romans 8:9). Though all who have received Christ are indwelt by the Spirit, not all are filled (empowered, motivated) by the Spirit.

The Holy Spirit:

a. Instructs us in all things.
b. Always glorifies Jesus Christ (John 25:26; 16:13-15).
c. Convicts us when things are wrong in our lives. (John 16:7-8).
d. Helps us to share Christ with others (Acts 1:8).
e. Assures us we belong to Christ (Romans 8:26).
f. Enables us to live above circumstances through prayer (Romans 8:26).
g. Flows from us as the source of an abundant and victorious life. (John 7:37-39).

HOW CAN YOU BE FILLED?

185

You can be filled (motivated) by the Holy Spirit right now IF YOU ARE WILLING to step off the mound of your life and give the ball to the Master Coach.

Now your attitudes and thoughts must all be constantly changing for the better. Yes, you must be a new and different person, holy and good. Clothe yourself with this new nature.

Ephesians 4:23-24

The Master Coach will not replace you on the mound against your heart's desire. Just as in receiving Christ, living consistently in His power is a matter of your will.

The Keys to Victory: Romans 6 (NAS)

A. KNOWING THIS, that our old self was crucified with Him that our body of sin might be done away with, that we should no longer be slaves to sin; for he who has died is freed from sin! (vs. 6-7)

B. Even so, CONSIDER YOURSELVES TO BE DEAD to sin, but alive to God in Christ Jesus. (v. 11)

C. But PRESENT YOURSELVES TO GOD as those alive from the dead, and your members as instruments of righteousness to God. (v. 13b)

PRESENT YOURSELF TO GOD THROUGH PRAYER

HERE IS A SUGGESTED PRAYER:

Dear Father,
I confess that I have taken control of my life and therefore have sinned against You. Thank You for forgiving me. I now CONSIDER myself dead to sin and PRESENT this body to You as a living sacrifice. I desire to be filled with Your Spirit as I live in obedience to Your WORD. Thank You for taking control of my life by the power of Your Spirit.

Amen.

HOW DO YOU KNOW YOU ARE FILLED BY THE HOLY SPIRIT?

> And we are sure of this, that He WILL listen to us whenever we ask Him for ANYTHING IN LINE WITH HIS WILL. And if we really KNOW He is listening when we talk to Him and make our requests, then we CAN BE SURE that He will answer us.
> I John 5:14-15

Is it God's will that you be filled (motivated) by His Spirit? He has said so (Ephesians 5:18). Therefore, based upon the authority of God's Word and His trustworthiness, you can KNOW you are filled with His Spirit regardless of your emotions.

WHAT IF SELF TRIES TO GET BACK INTO THE GAME?

The self life is a deadly enemy of the control of the Holy Spirit. Often self will try to return to the game, and when that happens, Satan quickly reloads the bases. If you sense this happening, take these steps:

1) Confess all known sin to God and thank Him. He has forgiven you (I John 1:9).

2) Trust Christ to again fill you with the Holy Spirit, who will once more take control (Ephesians 5:18).

WHAT WILL GOD'S PERFECT RELIEVER ACCOMPLISH IN YOUR LIFE?

He will retire all doubt, fear, worry and other sins that run the bases of your life. He will substitute love, joy, peace and other fruits (Galatians 5:22-23). His assortment of pitches includes truth, faith, righteousness and other weapons through which daily victory is assured (Ephesians 6:10-18). He will turn your eyes to the Master Coach, Jesus Christ, and conform you to His likeness (II Corinthians 3:18). You can praise and thank God through trials and suffering in the game of life, knowing He has a plan for you (James 1:2-4). The final score will bring much glory to God!

For further information, please write:

WINNING RUN FOUNDATION
4539 Artelia Drive
Antioch, TN 37013

THE WINNING RUN FOUNDATION

THE WINNING RUN FOUNDATION is a non-profit organization established for the purpose of publishing athletic-related devotional materials. The WRF materials listed below are now available through the Winning Run Foundation, 4539 Artelia Drive, Antioch, TN 37013:

THE WINNING RUN
A 16-page booklet using baseball diagrams to explain salvation in Jesus Christ. (Also available in Spanish)

THE PERFECT SUBSTITUTE
A 16-page tract using the game of basketball to illustrate salvation in Jesus Christ. (Also available in French)

THE WINNING STROKE
A 16-page booklet using the game of golf to illustrate salvation in Jesus Christ.

THE PERFECT SAVE
A 16-page booklet using soccer illustrations to explain salvation in Jesus Christ. (Also available in Spanish, French, Russian and Polish)

TEMPLE CONDITIONING
A 4-page tract detailing the Biblical basis for physical fitness.

WISDOM FROM THE MASTER COACH
A 32-page devotional using athletic illustrations to highlight the book of Proverbs.

SERMON ON THE MOUND
A 32-page devotional study of Matthew 5-7 using baseball terms.

MORE THAN WINNERS
An 84-page devotional using Olympic illustrations in a study of Romans - Revelation.

GROWING STRONGER
A 20-page, fill-in-the-blank Bible Study, containing memory verses and diagrams designed to help rookies in the faith to comprehend the basics of Christian living
(Also available in Spanish)

HIGH HURDLES FOR GIRLS
A unique 64-page Devotional/Bible Study of sixteen "hurdles" faced by the female athlete as she "runs the great race of faith."

THE POINT AFTER
A 136-page paperback published by Zondervan (1987). This book uses athletic illustrations to highlight God's dealings in the lives of His people in both Old and New Testaments.

OUR GREAT AND AWESOME GOD
A 180-page paperback published by Wolgemuth and Hyatt (1990), using athletic illustrations to highlight the goodness, the greatness and the names of God.

OUR GREAT AND AWESOME SAVIOUR
Another Wolgemuth and Hyatt (1991) release using athletic illustrations to glorify the life and message of the Lord Jesus Christ. (210 pages)

STRONG IN SPIRITUAL WARFARE
A 184-page paperback using athletic illustrations in a study of Spiritual Warfare. A current and timely topic!

TRIUMPH IN TRIBULATION
A perfect-bound paperback on Psalms. This book, filled with athletic illustrations, presents Jesus Christ as our Rock, our Fortress, and our Deliverer in the most trying circumstances of life.